A Shepherd Looks at the Lamb of God

Felise

15.03.15

A Shepherd Looks at the Lamb of God

W. Phillip Keller

A Pickering Paperback

First published by Bethany House Publishers 1982 under the title A Layman Looks at the Lamb of God.
This edition published 1983 by Pickering & Inglis, 3 Beggarwood Lane, Basingstoke, Hants RG23 7LP.

ISBN 0 7208 0527 9

Printed in Great Britain by
Spottiswoode Ballantyne Ltd, Colchester

The Author

W. PHILLIP KELLER is the author of 28 books, including: *A Shepherd Looks at Psalm 23, Rabboni,* and *Elijah: Prophet of Power.* Born in Kenya, East Africa, he studied in Canada to become an agrologist. The author is also a photographer, field naturalist, conservationist, and lay minister.

Other Books by W. Phillip Keller

Splendor from the Sea
As a Tree Grows
Bold Under God—A Fond Look at a Frontier Preacher
A Shepherd Looks at Psalm 23
A Layman Looks at the Lord's Prayer
Rabboni—Which Is to Say, Master
A Shepherd Looks at the Good Shepherd and His Sheep
A Gardener Looks at the Fruits of the Spirit
Mighty Man of Valor—Gideon
Mountain Splendor
Taming Tension
Expendable
Still Waters
A Child's Look at Psalm 23
Ocean Glory
Walking with God
Elijah—Prophet of Power
On Wilderness Trails
Salt for Society

Table of Contents

Introduction

"THE LAMB OF GOD. . . ."

What an unusual title! Among the countless varieties of animals, why was this particular species chosen most often to portray God's Son? What special significance does it bear?

Is it merely a picturesque pet name, or does it denote some profound truths about this person of divine origin?

Who *is* the One who bears this title? Why? From where does it come? To where does it lead?

These and a score of similar questions are generated by a study of this unique name, "*Lamb of God.*"

Strangely, yet significantly, He who alone wears this title entered into human history as The Lamb of God. Even the circumstances of His birth set the tone for this special name. He was born in a crude, contaminated, mideastern sheepfold outside Bethlehem.

This fact was driven home to me with intense and terrible force one day deep in the desert of Pakistan. I was in a remote village, alone, when suddenly a fierce, unexpected cloudburst and electrical storm drove me to seek shelter in a tiny mud-walled hovel. A very aged, white-bearded old man had beckoned me to come in out of the lashing fury of the storm.

Bending over deeply to crawl through the low

doorway, I fumbled my way into a dark and gloomy one-roomed abode. It took my eyes several minutes to adjust to the darkness within. The place was full of acrid smoke from a small dung fire burning between three cooking stones on the earthen floor. The air was fetid with the vile odors of livestock and sheep dung, for several of these animals shared the same tiny space.

In one corner, close by the fire, crouched the frail little form of a tiny, teenage girl, possibly the old man's daughter. Her large, luminous dark eyes were filled with a certain foreboding as she clutched a tender, newborn infant to her breasts. The baby whimpered slightly as the girl, wrapped about only with a soiled, threadbare, cotton cloak, rocked it gently in her thin arms.

Not knowing Pakistani, all I could do was huddle quietly, close to the smoky dung fire, while the storm beat upon the mud walls. Tiny rivulets of water ran down the dark walls where the rain leaked through the shabby roof.

Amid the gloom; amid the awful pungency of sheep, goat and other animal manure; amid the appalling poverty of this poor peasant's surroundings, God's Spirit spoke to me in unmistakeable, unforgettable terms: "*THIS is how I came amongst men!*"

The revelation came to my spirit with a force equal to the most ferocious thunder clap of the storm sweeping over this remote desert village. "O God, to what utter and absolute depths of privation and unspeakable pollution You descended to deliver us from our despair!"

All our fancy Christmas concerts; our pretty Christmas cards; our glowing lights; our glamorous paintings of the Nativity; our ornate gift packages; our tinsel and treats and trees—all these are but a travesty of the true conditions under which Christ came into the world.

Since that interlude, nearly twenty years ago, when I huddled in that desert shepherd's hut with a teenage mother and her suckling, newborn child, Christmas has never been the same again for me.

Those who first came to pay homage to that other newborn Babe in the Bethlehem stable were ordinary shepherds. In awe, wonder and simple faith they looked upon God's Lamb and were jubilant.

But wise men came, too, across the distant desert wastes of the then-known world. They came to honor and revere the Christ Child, the Prince of Peace, Heaven's Potentate, the Mighty God—yet also "The Lamb of God" in very truth (Isa. 9:6).

Beyond the simple shepherds, beyond the wealthy wise men, beyond the patriarchal priest Simeon and the aged Anna, who prayed so fervently for God's people, were His young mother, Mary, and her husband, Joseph. They also bowed low before this God-child. In this Lamb of God they glimpsed the salvation of God. In Him they recognized a Light which would give light to the entire Hebrew and Gentile world.

Some thirty years later the sturdy carpenter of Nazareth laid down His hammer and chisel for the last time. Crossing the countryside, He came to meet "the greatest man ever born of woman"—the fiery desert prophet, John the Baptist. As Jesus approached the blazing firebrand, whom one would have expected to point out qualities of strength and power, John exulted triumphantly, "*Behold, The Lamb of God, who taketh away the sin of the world!*"

This one, born in Bethlehem of Judea as foretold so accurately by the ancient prophets of His people, stood quietly before John and requested to be baptized in the Jordan. Not that He needed cleansing or absolution, but here He was distinctly identified with men in their human dilemma.

Later, looking upon this Christ, God's anointed One, there was torn again from The Baptist's innermost spirit the irrepressible declaration that *this man Jesus, is the Christ, The Lamb of God!* We will discover what it was in John's announcement which caused two of his own disciples to begin at that time to follow Jesus.

John the Baptist is one of many witnesses who answers our question, "Who is this One who bears the title, *The Lamb of God*?" Further on we will be considering others in Scripture who point eloquently and dramatically to Jesus, The Lamb of God.

There are six major word pictures, profound illustrations, in the Old Testament concerning The Lamb of God. We will look at each of these and at the unfolding picture of Christ himself provided in these passages.

Part One

The Lamb of God in Symbols

"Unto Adam also and to his wife did the Lord God make coats of skins, and clothed them" (Gen. 2:31).

Chapter One

Our Need for the Lamb

Adam and Eve's Necessary Covering

Mankind's need for The Lamb of God did not begin in a Bethlehem stable 2,000 years ago. Neither did The Lamb of God himself have His beginning there. The shepherd's stall was not His introduction into human history. The account of His initial entry into the world is but the narrative of that point in time when God, very God, chose to part the stage curtains of history behind which He had moved in majesty undetected by most to step out on center stage.

There in full view, The King of Glory, God in mufti, God disguised in human form, clothed and masked by our flesh and form, moved amongst men. Here was The *Lamb of God.* God's Son—in fact, God in person—had come to the lost sheep of men. He was unknown, unrecognized, but for a handful of men, humble in heart, receptive in spirit.

Indeed, this Lamb of God was none other than

the very person of the eternal God! He was the visible expression of the invisible God. He was the One who had been in company with the Father before ever the worlds were formed or the planet earth was shaped and fitted for human habitation.

He was The Lamb of God who, "from before the foundation of the world" (Rev. 13:8) was slain and suffered that men and women lost and perishing in the slime-pits of sin might be redeemed, reconciled and restored to walk with Him in paths of righteousness.

This concept of Christ as the ever self-sacrificing, ever self-giving One, yet very God himself, is one of the most difficult for us mortals to grasp. First, simply because we are finite. We are locked into and conditioned by our time/space limitations. As human beings we are born, live our little lives upon the planet, then perish. The few brief years of our short life span speed past us. The entire performance is like a swift dream that passes quickly from cradle to grave, as Shakespeare stated, "each man in his turn playing many parts." The idea of an eternal God—or even beyond that, an eternal *redeeming* God—is as elusive to our human understanding as the northern lights.

During these few years on earth, we are totally preoccupied with the pressing events of the immediate moment which touch upon our lives. We are naturally and inevitably preoccupied with survival amid the restless masses. We are driven inexorably to become self-centered, self-preoccupied in the scramble to succeed. And this is the second reason why it is so terribly difficult for us to envision, to grasp the love of God expressed so poignantly and profoundly in the person of His Son—the self-giving, self-sharing, self-sacrificing Lamb.

In fact, if anything, we recoil against such a concept. We see it as utter folly and foolishness. This sort of selfless love, of laying down one's life for another in need, of giving in order that others may gain, seems to us silly and absurd. In our hopeless cynicism and dark despair, we can scarcely conceive of a God who is gracious enough, good enough, generous enough, let alone great enough to go out of His way to give *himself* to save us from our sin.

But that is precisely what He does. It is what He always has done. It is what He always will do. He is the same eternal, unchanging, constant, compassionate Christ who from everlasting to everlasting lays himself out that man might live. And the few bright but painful years of His human sojourn are but a glimpse of His eternal performance in the unseen realm.

The remarkable revelation given to us mortal men by His own sublime Spirit is that of God, very God, dwelling and acting in the eternal dimension of the ever-present *now*. With Him there are no time/space limitations. With Him there is no restriction of space, no duration of days. With Him there is only the ever-present, ever-enduring I AM.

A thousand years with Christ is as one day and one day is as a thousand years. Even beyond this, a million milleniums are as one moment and one moment as a million milleniums. Because of this timeless quality, the unrestricted giving of God; the sharing of God; the sacrifice of God displayed for us in the central climax of Calvary is portrayed in the divine dynamic that meets the needs of uncounted millions upon millions of men and women for all time everywhere.

When in His own self-revelation, by His own Holy Spirit, God reveals to our recoiling spirits that He himself has been, is, and ever will be *The Lamb slain, The Lamb given, The Lamb shared, The Lamb who sacrifices himself in our stead,* we turn away from Him. It is more than our darkened souls and stony spirits can assimilate. Such a disclosure of the divine dimension cannot penetrate our sin-calloused souls. This is why the prophet cried out, "Who hath believed our report, and to whom is the arm of the Lord revealed?" (Isa. 53:1).

Yet the Scriptures from Genesis to Revelation are a record of God dealing with men in love and patience. From the first couple who communed with Him in the garden of Eden to the glorious city of eternal beauty revealed to the aged Apostle John, it is The Eternal Lamb who is portrayed for us. We poor, struggling, sinning mortals can scarcely comprehend this.

The recorded events depicted in the Bible speak eloquently and profoundly of this ever-suffering One. Long before earth was formed, God was gripped with grief and sorrow. This is the reason that Jesus is

"The Lamb slain from before the foundation of the world." For with His eternal foresight He acutely anticipated the agony and sorrow that would be His because of wayward man, "like sheep gone astray," turning to their own way, selling out completely to their strong-willed selfishness.

That such behavior would not only lead them to utter self-destruction but also would break in upon His own great love with enormous suffering of spirit would seldom occur to men. Blinded by the deception of the archenemy of their own souls, misled by the evil one and their own overwhelming preoccupation with sensuality, it would not dawn on them, or any of us, that it is our sin which has brought His suffering; it is our stupendous self-will which has caused His sorrow.

God made man for himself. He ordained, before ever earth was formed, that He should have sons and daughters with whom He could commune in pure delight. In the councils of eternity He determined that there should be those who would walk and talk and live with Him in intimate harmony.

Because of sin and evil, all this glorious plan was thrown into chaos and confusion. Every step God took to bring sons and daughters to glory was strewn with the sharp stones of His own suffering, the cutting wounds of His own great grief. We simply must see somehow, sometime, that God has suffered, *suffered,* SUFFERED, for us sinning people. This suffering has never diminished, either before or after Calvary.

Every significant illustration in the Old Testament

involving an earthly sacrifice is but a portrayal of the self-sacrifice borne by God himself.

When Adam and Eve deliberately, flagrantly asserted their own selfish desires to oppose God's best wish, His best will for them, He was pierced through with a thousand pains. These were but a foretaste of the iron spikes that would just as surely pierce His hands and feet, pinning Him to a cruel cross.

Men always do this to God. God has not changed; men do not change. Sinful men are still nailing God to the cross of their own conceit and indifference. They don't "give a dime" about what happens to Diety just as long as they can live as they like. It doesn't matter a whit to them if Christ does die a thousand deaths for their misdeeds.

For one who has spent countless hours enthralled with the beauty of God's creation, it stretches my imagination beyond its limits when I attempt to visualize the beautiful garden in which God placed the first man and woman. The Garden of Eden was both home and vocation for this pair. And even beyond the beautiful, soul-stirring environment and challenging, fulfilling occupation was their daily, unrestricted fellowship with *God himself!*

When Adam and Eve laid bare their own strong wills and did such despite to the loving care of their loving God, they stood stripped, naked and exposed in the gross ignominy of their shame. They were alienated from their Father. They were tasting the bitter fruit of their folly. Their end was death—spiritual, moral, physical death. They had brought it upon themselves. The personal loss to them is symbolized by the theological phraseology, the Fall of Man!

In amazing compassion and concern, God did not destroy them. He did not turn away from these two whom He himself had designed and created in selfless love. Instead, He suffered for their sakes. As a substitute for their punishment, God slew two innocent animals, most probably lambs, skinned them and clothed His earth children in their pelts.

Oh, how Adam and Eve *needed* that covering! They had to have it for their bodies, which had immediately begun to die and needed protection from the elements; for their minds, which were now handicapped by selfishness and were vulnerable to attacks from the enemy of their souls; and for their spirits, which were already dead from the moment of their sin, that could be made alive only through the redemption those two lambs represented.

With their willful, selfish choice, Adam and Eve laid the groundwork for that same choice by the myriads of their descendents all down through history. But it is not only Adam's sin that hurts God now; it is our own sinful thoughts, words, and deeds which "crucify the Lord afresh." This first sublime, significant sacrifice on earth to portray the suffering of the Lamb before the foundation of the world was a portrayal to Adam and Eve, *and to their offspring*, of the cost to God for their willful wrongdoing. Two innocent lambs had to die. Their blood had to be spilled. Their lives had to be laid down in order to provide a covering for the man and woman standing exposed in sin before a loving, caring, suffering God. The covering for Adam and Eve was a symbol of the covering necessary for the whole human race.

There was no inherent, intrinsic merit in the death of the lambs themselves. There was no spiritual efficacy in the warm, red blood that drained from their veins. There was no divine defense against the justice of God in the two skins now covering Adam and Eve. All the subsequent sacrifices that would ever be made upon earth, all the millions upon uncounted millions of lambs that ultimately would be slain upon thousands of altars in ages yet to come, were but a dim reflection of the unutterable remorse, sorrow, pain, and grief of a suffering Saviour.

Not all of these sacrifices combined could ever properly compensate for the sinfulness of man. The blood of lambs could never in itself make adequate reparation for the wretched attitudes and actions of the human race. What folly to ever feel it could! No indeed, a thousand times no—nothing that man could do would ever be able to make amends for his misdeeds against God. It was only, always, and ever will be *what God has done* that can suffice to pay the price. Only the laid-down life of God, the poured-out love of God, the pure and holy righteousness of God wrapped around our mortal souls could ever, ever atone for our dreadful behavior.

"...Abel was a keeper of sheep, but Cain was a tiller of the ground" (Gen. 4:2).

Chapter Two

No Substitute for the Lamb

Cain and Abel's Offerings

I have been both a "keeper of sheep" and a "tiller of the ground." Born and raised in Kenya, East Africa, to a Swiss family on a large country estate, I have always loved wildlife and the out-of-doors.

At the age of 18 I left home to attend the University of Toronto in Canada for training as an agrologist. My keen interest in all growing things was there nurtured and developed in preparation for the many years I later spent in agricultural research, land management and ranch development. So, in the area of crop production, and in the broader realm of the science of agriculture, I have been "a tiller of the ground." On the other hand, many aspects of my life as a sheep man, the time when I was a "keeper of sheep," have been shared with readers of *A Shepherd Looks at Psalm 23* and *A Shepherd Looks at the Good Shepherd and His Sheep.*

There is no sense in which these two occupations

of field husbandry and animal husbandry are not perfectly acceptable, satisfying and pleasing to God. The conjunction "but" used in the introductory Scripture passage is only for the purpose of contrast.

Both the sons of Adam and Eve had grown up with the knowledge and understanding of animal sacrifice. In their early years, this had been explained by their parents in very simple terms. But as they grew older, they received a clear, strong presentation concerning sin, its subsequent guilt, and the need for redemption from sin and guilt through the sacrifice of a lamb. At the time covered in this scripture portion, they had been instructed in the appropriate propitiation for their human wrongdoing and arrogant pride against God. Because of this spiritual training from their parents, both Cain and Abel now sensed that sacrifice of some sort must be made for their own misdeeds.

Though the true meaning of the sacrifice, the ultimate realization in Christ himself, was no doubt only a hazy picture far off in the future, Abel, the younger of the two boys, took this teaching very seriously. In careful solemnity he selected the choicest ram from his crop of lambs. With contrition, repentance, and in submission of his will, he killed the innocent creature, offering it as a substitute for himself, for his sin.

This is the first record of a human being's deliberate choice of God's appointed way for making appropriate atonement between himself and his God. It was not the slaying of the lamb which somehow earned God's favor, but it was the *One* whom that slain lamb represented which made this an action of implicit faith. Abel was saying, "O God, just as I have seen this little lamb's life laid down on my behalf, so I realize it represents Your life laid down in my stead." This simple shepherd offered the lamb to his loving God, confident it would be accepted because it portrayed in flesh and blood the divine life of The Eternal Lamb himself.

God looked on in love. He accepted the sacrifice. He was satisfied. Abel depended on God's generosity, not on his own good conduct. Here was the pattern for proper reparation for all men for all time. Their total dependence must be upon divine intervention, not on their own human effort.

Forgiveness, acceptance, acquittal, reconciliation between God and man could never be achieved by man's strivings, by man's manipulation. How could sinful, fallen man ever erase the wounds, dissipate the remorse, or undo the dreadful damage to God's gracious, generous nature? Even if it were possible for a person to "turn over a new leaf," to change his selfish direction by his own willpower, how could he erase the former years of sin and selfishness, the years of grieving a loving Heavenly Father? No, there is no way for the wrongdoer to redeem himself. The sin, the injury against God, needs the propitiation found only through the great Mediator himself.

This Abel realized. This Abel understood. This Abel acted upon in faith. This Abel saw as his only salvation. And thereby he was declared by God himself to be righteous, delivered from condemnation, cleansed from sin, and acquitted of the verdict against him. He was now accepted of God as a son.

Cain had received the same instruction, the same training from his parents as his brother Abel. He too should have understood the significance, the symbolism inherent in the death of a lamb for his sins.

It would seem from the Genesis account of this story that Cain surveyed his shepherd brother's sacrifice and arrogantly concluded, "Shepherd Abel has brought a lamb for sacrifice; I, Farmer Cain, will bring an offering representative of *my* vocation."

Everything about Cain's offering spoke of self-effort, self-interest, self-reliance. Nothing there even remotely portrayed the sacrifice of love poured out by God in His own self-giving for lost men as *The Lamb slain.* The fruit and grain came from the ground already cursed by God because of the intrusion of evil in the earth.

This concept of self-assertion was repeated in a tragic incident later on in biblical history when Moses broke the typology of Christ as the Living Water and "*smote* the rock" rather then speaking to it. Though the water did flow forth from the rock for the thirsty children of Israel, God had to deal severely with Moses for this breach of trust. He was not allowed to enter Canaan nor lead the Israelites on the final leg of their journey into the Promised Land.

To God, Cain's offering was an insult and injury. It was an affront. It was a destructive element in the second portrayal of Christ as The Lamb of God.

Cain's offering could not be accepted. It was an

attempt at self-merit and was of no value. Our human reasoning would cry out, "But Cain was *attempting* to please God; it was not as if he did not bring an offering at all!" From God's point of view, Cain's circumvention of His clear instructions concerning the sacrifice represented again the Fall of Man—man's pride, selfishness, independence, the turning "to his own way" to which Isaiah referred centuries later. In the very act of the offering, Cain was saying, "I will not bow to my Creator and Redeemer; I do not need the efficacy of the blood spilled." And, beyond this, Cain's arrogance had tarnished this eloquent picture of The Lamb slain in our stead.

Even so, the Scripture indicates that Cain could have even then brought a lamb offering to God, been forgiven and propitiated for his sin. But he hardened his heart against God and against his brother Abel; anger and jealousy mastered him; in the end, Cain became a murderer.

Now, thousands of years later, the implicit teaching in the story of Cain is that the cross of Christ cannot be circumvented. As the *need* for redemption is clearly seen in the story of Cain's parents, so the fact that *there is no subsitiute for Christ's redemption* is seen clearly in Cain's story.

"Take now thy son, thine only son Isaac, whom thou lovest, and get thee into the land of Moriah..." (Gen. 22:2).

Chapter Three

The Son Is the Lamb

Abraham's Test of Obedience

Perhaps only a father can truly understand the drama and pathos found in the story of Abraham and Isaac on Mount Moriah. My earliest memories of my own father, an American-Swiss layman whom God called as a missionary to East Africa, are shadowed by impressions of a tough, demanding man, though I had no doubt of his love for me. But later on, by the time I was in my teens, the Holy Spirit had worked in Dad's life, changing him into a truly caring, gentle, kindly person. He became a model, a pattern for my own responsibilities as a father.

I can only shake my head in awe and wonderment as I attempt to picture either Dad or myself in Abraham's position at the time of this Scripture passage. What an incredible test of love and faith!

A thousand years of time had passed since the symbolic offerings which were considered in the previous two chapters. Now God, again calling to Abraham with whom He had an intimate friendship and with whom He had previously spoken in direct and unmistakable ways, was clearly and categorically commanding the great desert nomad to take his son, the child of his old age, up to Mt. Moriah, "and *offer him there for a burnt offering*"!

Often God's people read His Word with questions or doubts about His true meaning, His real intent. "The Lord cannot *really* be saying anything quite so severe or stern." We hope that there is some other meaning, some "spiritual" interpretation which will "get us off the hook" and out from under responsibility for obedience.

It was almost as if the Lord was overstating His word to Abraham so that there would be no room for a shadow of doubt in his mind concerning God's instructions: ". . . thine only son Isaac, whom thou lovest. . . ." The relationship between Abraham and Isaac was very special, different than a usual father-son relationship. Isaac was the child of promise, son of Sarah's old age.

Perhaps thoughts of Ishmael, his firstborn, flashed through Abraham's mind. Though Abraham's love for Ishmael is in no doubt, would the test have been as profound, as poignant, if God had asked that Abraham's first son, the one he had had with Hagar, be sacrificed?

We can only imagine the kind of night Abraham spent after hearing God's word to him. Abraham could have been forgiven if he had waited a few days to be *sure* he had understood correctly, that this was not some dreadful mistake. But he "rose up early" the next morning, after having gotten little or no sleep, and without delay began his sorrowful mission. The dear old man must have died a thousand deaths as he and his son approached the mountain.

We have no indication that this special son Isaac had questions or was concerned that anything was amiss until the third day of travel. Abraham had seen the summit in the distance and instructed their two traveling companions to stay behind with the ass while "I and the lad go yonder and worship, and *come again to you*." There is no inkling here of a father's heavy heart or that there was any doubt concerning their return. But when Abraham laid the wood for the fire on Isaac, took a knife in one hand and fire for the altar in the other, and they had begun that long climb up Mt. Moriah, then Isaac said, "Father, we have the knife, the fire and the wood; *but where is the lamb*?"

Isaac had received the same spiritual training that Cain and Abel received; he knew that the appropriate sacrifice for this time of worship and communion with God was a lamb. Was this question he now addressed to his father purely academic, or did he sense something different about this offering? We can only guess at the thoughts going through Isaac's mind; but if he had fears, they were put to rest by Abraham's calm, simple rejoinder: "My son, *God will provide himself a lamb* for a burnt offering."

These words thunder down to us across the ages since that time, another thrilling reminder that the lamb sacrifice was not an invention of man's imagination to appease an angry God; rather, *God himself provides The Lamb!*

The faith of Abraham! His faith did not isolate him from asking God, "Why?" His mind was no doubt full of questions, and a band of anguish probably constricted his chest at times. But at rock bottom, Abraham's confidence in God's was steady and unwavering. We know from Hebrews 11:17 that Abraham believed that, if necessary, God would raise Isaac from the dead in order to carry out His covenant.

Abraham and Isaac arrived at the very same spot where later King Solomon was to build his marvelous temple to God. But the "point of no return" was fast approaching as father and son began laying up a rough altar of uncut stones. The physical exertion muted for a moment the pounding of this ancient patriarch's heart.

Then the altar was finished. Abraham laid on it the wood that would fuel the sacrificial fire. God could truly be relied upon to provide a substitute sacrifice for His son. The great Jehovah had done so for Adam and Eve. He likewise had accepted the lamb slain in simple trust by Abel. God would, now, again, intervene on behalf of him and his son Isaac.

No other sacrifice was in sight. Abraham took his beloved son, with burning, tear-filled eyes and trembling lips; bound him with rope and laid him upon the altar; he was ready to offer the dearest thing he owned in all the world to God.

His heart cried out, "I love my son, my son Isaac, whom you have given to me; but I love you more, Lord!" Abraham stretched forth his grizzled, sunburned hand to seize the knife that would slay his son, then a voice from heaven thundered: "Abraham! Abraham!" The patriarch's immediate answer was: "Here am I." His obedience to God was complete; whatever God's command, Abraham's response was that of a humble, obedient servant to the Lord.

"Do not lay your hand upon the lad," the voice commanded. "I know now that your faith and love for the Lord of glory, *The Lamb of God,* is unshakable since you have not withheld your son, your only son Isaac, from Me."

With racing pulse and beating heart, the old gentleman quickly released his son from the altar upon which he was bound. Lifting his eyes and looking around, he saw behind him a ram caught in a thicket by his horns; this ram became the burnt offering, the subsititute lamb for Isaac.

This mountain top of Mount Moriah would henceforth be called *Jehovah Jireh,* meaning "the Lord provides."

This dramatic story is not quite finished until we remember that there was heard a second voice from heaven that day. God's own father-heart fully understood the magnitude, the depth of Abraham's obedience. He was looking down through the centuries to that point in time when His own beloved Son would be the sacrifice for all men of all time. There would be no substitute then as there had been for Isaac; He was, is, and ever will be "*The Lamb of God* slain from before the foundation of the world."

Abraham's heavenly Father was moved by the expression of devotion from this earthly father, and God took this opportunity to reconfirm His covenant with Abraham. "In thy seed shall all the nations of the earth be blessed; because thou hast obeyed my voice."

And so The Lamb of God, the Lord of glory, accepted the substitute lamb as a proper and adequate provision for both the patriarch and his son. The ram lamb caught in the thicket at the right time, in the right place, for the right believers was a superb foreshadowing of the perfect provision of God's own suffering for His people.

This indeed the Lord had done—He himself was that Lamb.

This indeed Abraham believed—he took and trusted.

This indeed was counted to him for righteousness—he accepted God's substitute for his son.

"The blood shall be to you for a token upon the houses where ye are: and when I see the blood, I will pass over you..." (Ex. 12:13).

Chapter Four

The Passover Lamb

The Saving of the Firstborn

The Old Testament has been the stage setting in our unfolding drama of the Lamb of God. Act One in this divine drama took place in the Garden of Eden. Act Two was performed in the pasturelands around the rich Euphrates Delta. We saw Act Three on Mount Moriah. We have now come to one of the most gripping of the Old Testament scenes: Act Four occurs in the fertile lowlands of Egypt in the Delta of the Nile.

Nearly four hundred years have passed since that moving reprieve for Isaac on the mountain by Jehovah-Jireh himself. The Great Provider of a substitute for Abraham's child of promise had also provided a place of refuge for His people in the land of Egypt. I have considered with awe that area of land at the mouth of the Nile where the Hebrews made their homes. Approximately 100 miles long and 150 miles wide, it is a region of immense fertility. Even today this section of Egypt is a major factor to the nation in terms of crop production and livestock production.

The nation of Israel had been special, invited guests of the Pharaoh, probably Rameses II, to whom Joseph had been Vice Consul. Jacob's family, seventy strong, had come to make their home with Joseph during the famine. With some disdain, because they were livestock keepers, Pharaoh had generously assigned the Hebrews their own section of the country—the land of Goshen, the most fertile area of the whole of Egypt. It is no wonder that "the children of Israel were fruitful, and increased abundantly, and multiplied, and waxed exceeding mighty; and the *land was filled with them.*"

The status of these people had gradually deteriorated during the centuries after they left their homeland. "The king who knew not Joseph" was jealous and afraid of these "foreigners" whom God had so obviously blessed. He decided to use them for forced labor in his city-building projects. This only made them stronger, and their numbers increased further.

Eventually God's time for the great exodus of Israel from Egypt had come. The cruel Pharaoh, hating the Hebrews, yet greedy for their slave labor, was reluctant to release them. Plague upon plague was unleashed by God against the land of Egypt. Finally there would be a slaying of all the favorite, firstborn sons of every family. This was to be the last drastic judgment that would free Israel from their Egyptian slave masters. This great tragic event would signal the triumphal exodus of a whole nation, some two million people, from their bondage.

In order for God's special people, the Israelis, to be preserved from the awful peril of that night, each family was carefully instructed to offer a lamb or kid of the first year, flawless and unblemished, as a sacrifice. This lamb was to be known as the special "Passover Lamb." The laying down of its life, the shedding of its blood, the substitution of its flesh, would replace the death of each family's firstborn son.

Imagine the bustle and activity throughout the Nile Delta that day! The very best lambs of the Hebrew flocks were selected. Some families who were too few in number to use a whole lamb by themselves joined with neighbors and friends for the Passover celebration. The children were under watchful care that day. The firstborn son, particularly, was made to understand that his very life was being ransomed by the passover lamb. The mothers in each household prepared roasted flat cakes (Japatis) of unleavened flour. They prepared vegetables, the "bitter herbs," to be eaten with the roast lamb.

The lamb's blood was carefully collected in a bowl, then each Hebrew mother held the bowl as the father dipped a stalk of hyssop in the blood and applied it to the entrance of their home. The three applications on lintels and door jamb were symbolic of the cross. No doubt the oldest son watched this ceremony with great intensity and concern so every detail was in order. He probably checked several times later in the day to be sure that the blood was still clearly visible. The death of their own substitute lamb assured each family that the destroying angel would *pass over* that home. The lamb's blood sprinkled upon the doorposts and head cross-piece of the entrance way declared the immunity of the entire family within from the dire judgment without.

As evening came, every member of the family was carefully accounted for and kept indoors. They gathered around the table in traveling clothes, staves in hand, shoes on their feet. Quickly they ate the roasted lamb, herbs and bread. They were ready to leave in haste in the night.

As the hour of midnight came, the Hebrew families looked at each other in wonderment and awe as the Mideastern wails of mourning began to arise from the Egyptian households. "There was not a house where there was not one dead."

It was enough! God's predicted judgment was upon Egypt. Pharaoh could not wait to get the Israelis out of the land. "The Egyptians were urgent upon the people, that they might send them out of the land in haste; for, they said, We be all dead men" (Ex. 12:33).

God decreed that this Passover should be a memorial service, in memory of Israel's flight from Egypt—symbolic of The Passover Lamb Who was to come. There are three powerful emblematic elements in this service. The unleavened bread represented the haste with which the Hebrews left Egypt; it is also a picture of the sinless Christ, His body broken for us, of which we partake as members of His family. The bitter herbs represent the slavery, the misery which the Hebrews were leaving behind; these herbs also represent the bitter cup of suffering which our Lord drank in our behalf. The Passover lamb was the substitute, a sacrifice of shed blood providing protection from death for each Hebrew firstborn; this spotless lamb represented God's own firstborn, only begotten Son whose shed blood and laid-down life bears the death sentence for the whole world.

So, once more, in simple language and unmistakable symbolism, the lamb slain in Israeli homes in Egypt at that first Passover feast portrayed The Lamb of God, slain from the foundation of the world—the One Who 1,500 years later would be offered in death at the Passover feast in Jerusalem.

The authenticity and accuracy of this portrayal comes with special impact to those of us who through force of circumstances or choice of profession have had to slaughter sheep. During my own years as a sheep rancher, the so-called "killing season" was a time of personal anguish and remorse. Yet the slaughter of lambs was absolutely essential to the success of the ranch operation itself; some lambs simply had to be sacrificed every year in order for the rest of the flock to flourish and thrive. The flock had to be kept to a size that the ranch could support in terms of optimum nourishment, shelter and disease control. My own survival as a shepherd depended directly upon the substitute death of my own lambs.

This was no easy thing for me—no light task; no

careless, casual incident. The little creatures are so silent in the hands of their owner. They do not bleat or scream in protest. It is almost as if they quietly acquiesce to their own death. As the killing knife severs the jugular vein from which the warm lifeblood flows, there is not a sound. The little, innocent life, lived so briefly, so fleetingly, for a few months, is poured out in but a few brief moments.

They are born to die!

They came briefly but for this one purpose.

Out of their death springs life for others!

A profound principle little understood by most Christians and seldom explained, because it is never fully grasped, is the law of the so-called "energy conversion cycle," a term used in scientific circles. If I am able to explain this in understandable terms, it will enable the reader to recognize how authentic and realistic is the divine revelation of God's Word.

Once death had entered into the dimension of life upon planet Earth, it began to condition all of its activities. This was not God's original intention. Our federal parents, Adam and Eve, were endowed with the same enduring, eternal life as God himself. But this was short-circuited and grounded to earth because of their submission to Satan. They believed his insinuation that willful disobedience to God was really of no grave consequence or significance.

When Adam and Eve set their own selfish wills in direct opposition to that of their loving Heavenly Father—this Creator who had given them a wonderful environment, fulfilling occupation, His own friendship, His very life—an incredible separation occurred.

The self-centeredness of man was set against the selflessness of God. Evil and good, death and life, despair and love—the darkness of man's dilemma and the light of God's salvation were set in direct opposition one to the other. Because of this death, because of this separation, God's best plans were perverted. The sentence of death had been passed on man and all other forms of life. Life no longer came from God directly to His creation; life would now come through death.

Allow me to explain. Rather than our first parents partaking freely and fully of abundant resources provided for them directly from the hand of God, they now had to turn and till the soil and husband livestock. Every crop they produced, whether from their little garden or their little flock, would have to forfeit its life in order to feed and sustain man.

Life could now come to them only through death—the death of grain, vegetables, fruit, flesh or food of any sort that once possessed life.

In short, one life had to be laid down for another life. One needed to die in order for another not to die.

This principle prevails to this very moment. Every erg of energy we possess, every ounce of weight our bodies carry, every element of life we own is ours only by virtue of the death of other living forms.

God instantly saw and knew all this the moment Adam and Eve sinned. He recognized at once the rupture of His own wonderous original design and intentions for man. And God immediately initiated His own intervention, the plan He had already prepared, to redeem us from this human dilemma. The first innocent lambs were slain, and their pelts provided the first couple with protection from the elements, flesh for survival, and atonement for their sin.

Even further, this substitutionary sacrifice was a signal from God to man that He knew all life on earth was henceforth conditioned and dependent on death. The energy conversion cycle was already underway. All life thereafter would come only through death.

God knew that ultimately only the forfeiture of His own divine life could possibly provide the eternal life essential to man's survival. Only from His divine death could come our hope of immortal life. The Creator had given life once; now, through death, He was giving it again. This is why every lamb ever offered, every sacrifice ever made, every life of an animal forfeited was a special symbol of God's own redemptive purposes. True, these animals were offered as a substitute for the owner himself; but, beyond this, they depicted this profound principle that governs and pervades the entire human race—that life comes only through death.

The liberal theologians who look with disdain upon what they refer to as the "butcher-shop" gospel show an enormous naiveté in failing to understand this combined scientific and spiritual principle at work in the universe.

It is noteworthy that in giving the clearly defined

instructions to the Hebrews for their preparation of the Passover lamb, God emphatically told them to consume its flesh in entirety that night. Not only would the blood of the lamb sprinkled on the doorposts provide them with protection from judgment, but the flesh of the lamb eaten that night would energize them to escape from Egypt and "pass over" the Red Sea to freedom.

Some 1,500 years later, *The Passover Lamb* arrived in Jerusalem at the time of the Passover Feast. He wished to celebrate this special memorial service with His friends.

On that night, the twelve young men little knew the enormous significance of their simple meal together with the Master. They were still quarrelling and wrangling over personal position. They were still at odds over jealous rivalries. One of them, a ruthless and selfish thief, was totally oblivious to the Passover supper as either a memorial or a sacrament.

As Judas took the broken bread and poured-out wine from His Saviour's hands, he had no idea those same hands would soon be nailed to a cross. Preconceived ideas of power and wealth had blinded his view of Christ as *God's Lamb.* The rest of the group were really not much better. Those who did meditate on the first Passover celebration were ignorant of *The Passover Lamb* in their midst. They did not realize that in a few short hours, Jesus would be offering himself as the supreme sacrifice for all men of all time. They did not know that as every lamb offered on ten million altars had looked forward to this point in history, so from then on every Communion service held, every Last Supper celebrated, would look back to it. But there was One at that table who knew, who fully understood what was facing Him as if it had already taken place.

Not only would that life laid down in our behalf provide a substitute for our sins, but also that body broken and spilled blood shared with us would provide the very life essential to our eternal survival.

This was the issue to which Christ addressed himself so emphatically in John 6 and the one which even His closest disciples had difficulty accepting: "Except ye eat the flesh of the Son of man, and drink his blood, ye have no life in you. Whoso eateth my flesh, and drinketh my blood, hath eternal life; and I will raise him up at the last day" (John 6:53, 54).

The Lamb of God, *The Passover Lamb* slain in our stead, was a spotless Lamb. He was not stained with His own wrongs. He was not contaminated by His own selfishness, His own willfulness.

It was our sin, our selfishness, which He took upon himself. He, who knew no sin at all, condescended to be made sin for us that we might be made right and clean and pure with the righteousness of God.

It is significant that in the original ordinance established by God for the sacrifice of the Passover lamb, clear, unmistakable details were given for the total disposal of the animal. Its blood was to be sprinkled on the doorposts, its flesh was to be eaten, and all the rest—the pelt, fleece, wool, and offal— were to be consumed by fire before dawn.

This fire represents divine retribution and judgment upon the parts of the animal not consumed by the family. At Calvary that same inviolate judgment fell upon our sins, our selfishness, our wrongs, our pride—all borne in the person of our suffering Saviour. In appalling agony and spiritual separation from God himself, our Lord endured the awesome ignominy of hell in order that we might be spared, saved... *passed over*... by the irrevocable judgment of our righteous God.

"The goat, on which the lot fell to be the scapegoat, shall be presented alive before the Lord, to make an atonement with him, and to let him go for a scapegoat into the wilderness" (Lev. 16:10).

Chapter Five

The Sin-Bearing Lamb

The Scapegoat in the Wilderness

History moves on. Israel has celebrated the first Passover and has left Egypt en mass. The great exodus of an entire nation, at least two million strong, has taken them across the upper reaches of the Red Sea into the desert wastes of Sinai—the Mount of God. And here we come to Act Five. Three months after Act Four has taken place in Egypt, Act Five in the divine drama is performed in the wilderness.

It is difficult to describe in words the forbidding solitude but majestic grandeur of this desolate setting. Certainly there would be no distractions of civilization as God prepared to speak directly and personally to His special servant Moses and, through him, to His people. Imagine the numbing awe of the children of Israel, after their careful ceremonial cleansing and after the fearful warnings against untimely approach to the mountain, to see their leader, their father-figure, Moses, disappearing into the thunderous cloud.

On this gaunt and dreadful mountain, God gave to Moses not only the Ten Commandments, the basic structure for the moral and ethical conduct of God's special people, but also detailed instructions as to how these Ten Commandments should be lived out in their daily lives. At this point in time, these instructions were bound up with symbolic ceremonies and specific sacrifices which were important to the whole nation. With their limited spiritual understanding and without a written Word of God, they needed these visual ceremonies.

Though God chose to speak to His people through these graphic celebrations, He never intended the symbol to replace personal faith and wholehearted obedience to His commands. "This people honoreth me with their lips, but their heart is far from me . . . for laying aside the *commandment* of God, ye hold the *tradition* of men, as the washing of pots and cups: and many other such like things ye do" (Mark 7:6-8).

Among the instructions given to Moses on Mount Sinai were details for a special ceremony to be included with the burnt offering. It would be a dramatic visual presentation to Israel of God's unique work in atonement. Combined with the sin offering described in Leviticus 16, there was to be a second animal "presented alive before the Lord" which would bear away the sin of the people.

The two kid goats were necessary to fully describe the two aspects of the work which Christ would complete on the cross. The High Priest, Aaron, had specific instructions concerning his ceremonial cleansing and attire. Then he was to select from the flock of Israel two matched kids, healthy and unblemished. Aaron was to cast lots on the two, selecting one for a sacrifice to God and the other for a scapegoat. The first animal symbolized the atonement for sin which was needed in order for Israel to have fellowship with God; the second one represented that which the sin-bearing Lamb of God would do at Calvary: *bear in His own body* the sins of the whole human race, taking them away, to be remembered against us no longer.

Again, the symbolism of this sacrifice and ceremony was a clear reflection to the whole nation of their atonement. In subsequent centuries, the millions of lambs, kids, and bullocks slaughtered and sacrificed on the altars of Israel were speaking of God in Christ, The Lamb suffering in their stead and bearing away their sins.

These sacrifices of blood certainly looked forward to the culmination of all such offerings when Christ himself would fulfill the picture; but they looked back, as well, to all that had been accomplished already by God for them in His suffering and agony on their behalf. Even thousands of years before the fact, Christ's death was a *fait accompli;* God suffered through every animal sacrifice as if He were suffering on the Cross already.

This peculiar people, chosen to carry out God's special plan for the world, had grieved and wounded

Him beyond our ability to comprehend. Their parting comment as Moses left them to talk face to face with God was, "All that the Lord has spoken, we will do." Yet when Moses returned to the people from the mountain, he faced a scene of lawlessness and lewdness beyond imagination. Again and again throughout their history, rebellion, stubborness, waywardness and perverseness cost Him enormous pain and suffering.

The great poets and prophets of Israel spoke often of the suffering Saviour. David, the ancient shepherd king of Israel, spoke both poetically and prophetically of God's Son enduring great shame and suffering.

In his magnificent Psalm 22, speaking under the inspiration of God's own Spirit, he portrays in clear and powerful passages the suffering of God, very God in Christ—*The Lamb of God.* In moving stanzas, David looking down the years, was quoting Christ "before the fact": "My God, my God, why hast thou forsaken me?" What a shattering, sobering thought that Christ himself should be forsaken! That, for no sin on His own part, He should endure such terrible separation from His Father.

The hymnwriter of a past century has caught the drama and pathos of this sin-bearing Lamb so well:

O Lamb of God! Thou wonderful sinbearer;
Hard after Thee my soul doth follow on;
As pants the hart for streams in desert dreary,
So pants my soul for Thee, O Thou life-giving One.

I mourn, I mourn, the sin that drove Thee from me,
And blackest darkness brought into my soul;

Now, I renounce th' accursed thing that hindered,
And come once more to Thee, to be made fully whole.

Descend the heavens, Thou whom my soul adoreth!
Exchange Thy throne for my poor longing heart,
For thee, for Thee, I watch as for the morning;
No rest or peace is mine from my Saviour apart.

Come, Holy Ghost, Thy mighty aid bestowing,
Destroy the works of sin, the self, the pride;
Burn, burn in me, my idols overthrowing,
Prepare my heart for Him—for my Lord crucified.

At Thy feet I fall, yield Thee up my all,
To suffer, live, or die for my Lord crucified.

The powerful portrait of the sacrificial lamb is not one which appeals to our human vanity and pride. Mankind shuns suffering. We abhor humiliation. We flee from sorrow of any sort. Degradation and despair are conditions we resist.

And yet the human condition, despite all our fancy pretense at success and splendor, is shot through with pathos and pain. Life itself, as C. S. Lewis so provocatively points out, carries much more pain than pleasure. The tapestry of our days is colored more strongly with stress than with singing, it is woven through with dark threads of despair and grief more than with strands of glory and light.

The human mind rejects the implications of God himself suffering for our salvation; yet if *God* suffers, how can puny man escape it? In all our frantic efforts to escape suffering, do we realize that our own sin and selfishness are the cause of so much suffering in this life and in the hereafter?

In chapter 59 of his prophecy, Isaiah gives a graphic description of the human condition with this opening statement: "Your iniquities have separated between you and your God, and your sins have hid his face from you, that he will not hear." And the prophet goes on to describe man in his folly and childish reactions, shaking his puny fist at his Maker. Cyncial and skeptical, he tries to cover his inner despair and soul sickness with a smirk or a smile. He pretends all is well when, in fact, all is wrong within.

His are the symptoms of a grief that eats away his soul like an insidious gangrene. He is out of touch with God, out of joint with his fellowman, and, even more often, alienated from himself. In anguish he wanders on, sometimes longing for light, more often preferring the darkness of his own evil deeds. We resent and resist this disclosure of our own undone condition. We insist in our selfish pride that "mankind is not so bad." We cling to the false hope that mankind is getting better and better.

It is no wonder that Isaiah concluded, "there was no man [to help], and wondered that there was no intercessor" (Isa. 59:16). But the prophet did not stop there: "*therefore HIS arm brought salvation. . . .*"

There was no help for man, except God himself step into our time and space. Before ever a race of men set foot on this planet, The Lamb of God was prepared, in case it was necessary, to come and bear away their total grief and sorrow, these outer symptoms of the inner illness of sin and selfishness which is the bottomless chasm separating us from God and from our fellowman.

Somehow, somewhere, someone must build a bridge across that appalling chasm. We cannot save ourselves, try as we may. We cannot cleanse our own conscience. We cannot shrug off our own sin. There must be a sinbearer apart from ourselves.

This God has always seen and clearly understood. *Man has not!*

And so here in the wilderness at Mount Sinai, God added a bold, fresh stroke to the portrait of The Lamb of God. The two young animals before the High Priest represented another piece in the unfolding picture of God's atonement. After the lot was cast and the one was chosen for the sacrifice, its blood was carefully brought into the innermost holy place of the tabernacle to be sprinkled on the mercy seat where God met with man. Instead of suffering for their own sins, absolution and atonement were made through the death of the lamb for the entire nation.

The eternal law, the inviolate principle, that "the soul that sinneth, it shall die," had been fully exonerated. In the substitute death of another, the law was satisfied and the guilty sinners set free.

Further evidence and illustration of this incredible transaction was now ready for public manifestation with the second sacrificial kid. This was to be a public demonstration to the rest of the nation, barred from entrance to the holy of holies, that their sins had in fact been forgiven. This was public assurance that their God had met them in mercy. They could now know beyond doubt that their guilt was gone and their future was free.

His hands already stained with the lifeblood of the first animal, the High Priest now laid them upon the head of the second little innocent creature, symbolic of the transfer to it of all the sins of Israel.

This sacrificial animal, too, would pay with its life. The sinbearer scapegoat would carry away the sins of the nation into the oblivion and obscurity of the wilderness. Led away by a "fit man," representative of the only One truly appropriate for this task, this little animal would never be seen again.

This was an annual rite, a symbolic and visual demonstration once each year to the nation of Israel of the two messages inherent in the atonement.

Years later in Israel's history, the Spirit of God speaking through the inspired writer to the Hebrews declared categorically that the blood of goats and lambs could never take away sin, "for the law *having a shadow* of good things to come, and not the very image of the things, can never with those sacrifices which they offered year by year continually make the comers thereunto perfect . . . But *this man*, after he had offered one sacrifice for sins for ever, sat down on the right hand of God" (Heb. 10:1, 12).

Christ fulfilled all the parts of this ceremony when He died on the cross—He himself is the great High Priest, the sacrificial Lamb, the "fit Man" and the Scapegoat bearing away our sins into the immensity of God's generous forgetfulness!

In turn, for all He has borne on my behalf, He asks only that I reach out my hands in faith and lay them in quiet trust upon His person. Just as the priest in faith placed his hands on the living animal which would be led away into the wilderness, so now I can rely upon my divine Sinbearer to act for me. Christ's assurance to me is that if I do so, my sins will be borne away, never more to be remembered against me. "I will put my laws into their hearts, and in their minds will I write them; and their sins and iniquities *will I remember no more*" (Heb. 10:16, 17). What deliverance! What freedom!

Even beyond His wonderful forgiveness and acceptance, the Father invites us to enter now *with boldness* into the holiest by the blood of Jesus. A child of God can have this confidence because of the ministry of the divine Scapegoat. Under the protection of God's divine forgetfulness, we can in turn forgive and accept others; and we can even forgive ourselves. We then know what it is to walk in the light, the wonderous brightness of His presence. Our days have meaning. Our years have purpose. Our despair has turned into the laughter of a joyous love—love for God; love for other followers of the Lamb; love for the lost.

"Surely he hath borne our griefs, and carried our sorrows; yet we did esteem him stricken, smitten of God, and afflicted. But he was wounded for our transgressions, he was bruised for our iniquities: the chastisement of our peace was upon him, and with his stripes we are healed. All we like sheep have gone astray; we have turned every one to his own way; and the Lord hath laid on him the iniquity of us all. He was oppressed, and he was afflicted, yet he opened not his mouth: he is brought as a lamb to the slaughter, and as a sheep before her shearers is dumb, so he openeth not his mouth" (Isa. 53:4-7).

Chapter Six

The Suffering Lamb

Isaiah's Word Pictures of the Lamb of God

This is an appropriate point in this study of the Lamb of God to reflect on the historical sequence of Isaiah's special revelation. Much of the enormous impact of this passage from Isaiah lies in its prophetic accuracy. Not only does the prophet picture the ritualistic rites of the Passover lamb slain on ten million Israeli altars for the preceding 700 years, but also he depicts under the inspiration of God's Spirit the suffering of God's own Passover Lamb some 700 years in the future.

We have come to the sixth sublime Act in the ongoing pageantry of God's revelation of himself as our Saviour. The suspense, the drama, has been building with each new presentation of the Lamb of God. The first five gave to God's people important aspects of what the Lamb of God does. Now, Isaiah, seven centuries before the fact, paints in stirring language, which only God himself could have inspired, a vivid description of The Lamb of God himself.

Now we see lifted up, for all men of all time, the Lamb slain, not only for His own chosen people but for the *whole human race.* "*All* we like sheep have gone astray; we have turned everyone to his own way; and the Lord hath laid on him the iniquity of us *all*" (Isa. 53:6). It is with the sheep who have gone astray that The Lamb of God, though spotless and having never strayed himself, is so strongly identified. The blind, selfish, groping sheep can be brought into the fold only by The Lamb of God.

God has never left man in ignorance or confusion concerning His purposes. All through the long prelude of centuries prior to His own appearance, The Lamb of God acted decisively, deliberately to reveal in unmistakable terms that every move He made, every action He took was for His lost sheep, His lost people.

Who Believes Our Report?

The simple, clear answer to the prophet's rhetorical question is, *almost no one!*

The reason, of course, is obvious. We do not believe the prophet's presentation of the problem nor the solution to our human dilemma. We assume rather naively that most of us are a rather respectable lot. How quickly do we forget the appalling atrocities which man has perpetrated against man, and against God, all down through human history.

We deliberately close our eyes to the never-ending tragic tale of death, murder, greed, cruelty, theft, rape, torture and war which have marked man's footsteps from the murder of Abel to the killing of millions of the unborn today. We tend to believe for the most part that human beings are noble, grand and glorious individuals, intent only on lofty ideals and righteous aspirations.

Too often in our western culture, with its history of Judeo-Christian influence, we forget the ferocious pagan conduct of the hidden peoples who have known nothing of God and His incredible love. Modern humanists with their secular philosophies often hold forth on the "essential goodness of man"—as if primitive societies are happy, free, innocent children at heart. This is in spite of the evidence of cruel, heartless cultures and cults; the atrocities of inter-tribal wars and vendettas; the casual attitude toward human life; the human sacrifices; the torture of children—the list could go on and on and should stab us wide awake to the dilemma of those who grope about in the darkness of unbelief.

But, no, mankind does not believe the prophet's report about the human condition; neither do we believe the prophet's report concerning God's way out of man's dilemma. That God himself should take on a body "marred more than any man," to be despised and rejected by the very ones to whom He came, take more than human understanding to comprehend. We are still hiding our faces from Him.

Is it any wonder, then, that when God came among us in human guise, He was tortured to death—offered as a human sacrifice, the final horror of our human degradation?

We dare not look with righteous disdain upon those contemporaries of Jesus who crucified Him so long ago. Cruelty and hatred and injustice and flaming fury are not the special hallmark of a certain passionate race of another generation. Twentieth-century man, with his sophisticated, smooth, cynical veneer of civilization, is no less a part of that roaring mob which led Him away to be crucified.

This deeply moving proclamation by Isaiah is not one man's view of the human dilemma, but God's. Whether Isaiah's report is believed or not changes not one iota of its truth.

For reasons not clearly understood by Bible scholars, Isaiah's prophetic utterances regarding Christ's sufferings have been broken arbitrarily in two at the beginning of chapter 53. Some translators from the past have actually incorporated Isaiah 52:13-15 into chapter 53. At the very least, the last verses of chapter 52 should be looked upon as the preamble and overture to this magnificent portrayal of the suffering Lamb.

Isaiah cries out that the eternal God comes disguised as the suffering Servant. He will succeed in His magnificent mission of seeking and salvaging lost sheep. By the incredible exchange of laying down His life for ours, He is able to raise us from our ruin.

Oh, that we could grasp the import of that phrase, "laying down his life"! In our beautiful sanctuaries and comfortable pews, we tend to forget that

His royal visage is marred and contorted beyond recognition. He who has never known even a moment's fleeting whisper of personal guilt carries the guilt of every man, woman, and child who has ever lived . . . —"the Lord hath laid on him *the iniquity of us all.*"

Evil men mocked and jeered at his death. Satan and his cohorts laughed fiendishly at their seemingly successful conspiracy. They thought they had killed God! They thought they had thwarted His best plan. They concluded for a moment that the King's Representative was no longer a factor to be dealt with.

But the presumptuous victory orgy turned to terrified silence as indications of divine wrath were unleashed upon the earth. The three hours of darkness at noonday were sobering enough; but the veil of the temple rent from top to bottom; the earthquake; the exploding rocks; the opened graves; and appearances of those long dead caused even the godless soldiers to conclude, "Truly this was the Son of God!"

Hand-in-hand with evil men, the father of evil had had only a fleeting moment of triumph. From before time began, *God had planned* for the death of His Son. The forces of darkness had actually cooperated in their own undoing! Because the cross is not the culmination of God's redemption plan. Beyond it lay a royal mausoleum. Christ's death was but a step towards the Resurrection morning. That which to the onlookers appeared as a total tragedy was and is a perpetual triumph in the economy of eternity.

Isaiah caught a glimpse of that triumph in the closing refrain of Isaiah 52: "Many nations will marvel at him. Kings will be speechless with amazement" (Isa. 52:15, GNB).

Yet in spite of all the foregoing good news, most men and women simply will not believe in Him, the One who made intercession for the transgressors.

The word *believe* is commonly bandied about in Christian circles. We use the phrase "believe in Christ" very casually and sometimes carelessly. We speak glibly about thousands, if not millions, of so-called believers.

What does the word "believe" as used in Scripture really mean? Giving mental assent? Accepting an idea as true? Giving credence to the concept of an historical Christ?

To simply accept that He was born in Bethlehem, lived and ministered among men for thirty-three years, then died a dreadful death on a cruel Roman gibbet is not *believing*, in the spiritual dimension of the word. Even millions of Moslems believe in Jesus Christ this way.

Our Lord himself when He was here on earth had trouble getting people to really believe. He decried the fact that though He spoke to them about himself, though He taught them truth clearly, though He performed mighty miracles, they still did not truly believe (John 10:24-38).

To believe means that one has a deep inner passion (thirst) for Jesus Christ which can be satisfied only by partaking of His own life and Spirit. "Jesus said unto them, I am the bread of life; he that cometh to me shall never hunger; and he that believeth on me shall never thirst" (John 6:35, 36). In the next chapter of John, on the last day of the great feast, "Jesus stood and cried, saying, If any man thirst, let him come unto me, and drink. He that *believeth* on me, as the scripture has said, out of his belly shall flow rivers of living water" (7:37, 38).

In the realm of our physical well-being, if we thirst, we must drink water. Our bodies are roughly 70% liquid. In order to maintain cell turgidity and for body metabolism to proceed normally in good health, water must be assimilated into our systems daily; water is essential in order to sustain the chemical and physical exchanges of nutrition as planned. Likewise, in the spiritual sense, to believe implies that the very life of God in Christ must be assimilated into our spirits, into our souls. We must actually open our innermost being to receive Him. We then become partakers of the very nature of God himself.

The result of this kind of *believing* will be a diametric change in us. We are no longer just men and women who know about an historical Jesus. We are no longer those who merely discuss a doctrinal Christ in a casual, clinical way. We will no longer regard God as a distant deity, detached and far away from us in the immensity of outer space. Christ becomes the very source of our life, our constant companion. His presence by His Spirit is a living, dynamic reality. His will, His wishes, His intentions, His purposes become ours. He is the confidante for all our decisions. We know Him, and we are acutely, serenely aware that He knows us. In brief, *to believe* in Christ is to have Him as part of every moment, waking or sleeping.

"God gave us eternal life, and this life is in his Son. He who possesses the Son has that life; he who does not possess the Son of God does not have that life" (1 John 5:11, 12, AMP).

A moment's reflection will make abundantly clear to us that the number who have believed the prophet's report this way are remarkably few—perhaps less than 5% of the earth's total population. Our Lord warned us that it would be so. Few there be who find this life, this truth, this way to live. But it is to this tiny handful that the arm of the Lord is revealed. It is to them that God in Christ becomes a powerful person. The Spirit of God becomes their companion, their counselor, their comrade-in-arms for their sojourn here on earth.

It is the one who is prepared to accept God's evaluation and verdict regarding his own undone condition who will turn to Christ. No longer holding God at arm's length, and now seeing himself in his own sin and despair, he will open himself to Christ's entry into his life. To this one the Saviour comes, revealing himself in all of His winsome compassion, understanding and strength. With forgiveness, acceptance, love and serenity, He becomes our dearest friend, our fondest companion. It should not be difficult then to concede quickly to His lordship of our lives. He deserves to be sovereign. He is entitled to hold preemminence in our affairs.

This is to recognize, "O Christ, you are God, very

God." This is to respond, "O Christ, your wish is my command." This is to reply, "O Christ, whatever You wish, I shall do it." Herein lies peace—Christ in us. Herein lies power—Christ through us.

The Lambkin's Tender Years

Under the inspiration of God's own gracious spirit, the prophet Isaiah proclaims in the second verse of this remarkable chapter that the coming one, the Christ, the suffering one, would grow up as a "suckling," a "tender shoot," a "tiny lambkin."

The Hebrew expression used here is YONEQ, derived from the verb YANAQ, which in its most profound intent refers to a small, nursing infant or a suckling, newborn offspring.

Most ancient translators have represented this term as a tender young shoot, a frail sprig of new growth emerging from a stump growing in a waste piece of desert land.

But it can also mean a little lambkin whose heel marks—hoofprints—are made in dry, dusty ground. For the Hebrew term SHORESH, generally interpreted as "root," can also mean "heel." Both word pictures are valid, though the second is more in keeping with the over-all theme of this magnificent pronouncement. Nor does it change the metaphor.

This Lamb would grow up before the Lord, not in lush surroundings befitting His origins, but in the "desert"—in very humble, ordinary circumstances. His family had only the most meager of material possessions; His education paralleled that of an ordinary Jewish boy. His occupation was that of a carpenter, working with His hands to fashion things for others to use.

This tender Lambkin did not gambol through verdant green pastures divided by a sparkling mountain stream; his heelprint was found in the desert places, unlikely surroundings to produce and nurture the very Son of God.

This one took upon himself the form of a servant, made himself of no reputation, and was made in the likeness of men (Phil. 2:7). Born in a sheepfold to a carpenter's wife and raised in the hot, dusty market town of Nazareth in the province of Galilee which was looked upon with disdain by the rest of the country, the Eternal One, the Mighty God, the Prince of Peace became in fact God's tender Lambkin. He it is who would become a suffering servant but also our sinless substitute.

Our Suffering Substitute

It is proper and appropriate at this point to remind the reader that this One who stooped down to become the suffering substitute Lamb of God for our sakes will one day also stand before us in unbelievable splendor, majesty and light as the supreme Judge of all the earth.

We do well to remember that sin, particularly our own sins, are not easily set aside by God. Sin is totally abhorrent to Him. He does not casually "sweep them under the carpet." The immutable law of God has been broken; a penalty must be paid. When God pays that penalty, and we accept His substitutionary death as our own, we are brought into a new relationship: the judge has become our father.

This is the reason that to reject the great Judge's offer is such a heinous crime. This is why those who cling to their sins, their own way, rejecting God's gracious offer, are "crucifying the son of God afresh."

Some years ago a young woman was arraigned before a California court for a misdemeanor. When the charge was read, she pleaded guilty. All the evidence and her own conscience pointed to a verdict of guilty.

It was no surprise when the judge, in sonorous tones, read out the verdict against her. She had to either pay a fine of $100.00 or spend ten days in jail.

Unfortunately, the youthful offender did not have the money to discharge her debt. She was helpless to free herself from the judgment against her.

The judge looked down at her in the prisoner's dock. There she stood, totally guilty before the law. Her own waywardness had led her into this awkward predicament.

Slowly, surely, with great dignity, the judge slipped his robes from his broad shoulders. In a gesture of momentous consequence, he stepped from behind the bar and came down the steps to stand beside his own daughter in the dock.

Reaching into his own pocket, he withdrew the amount of money needed to cancel her debt, paying the price to set her free.

He who had been her judicial magistrate had also been her loving father. It was he who paid the full penalty of her crime, and it was he who stamped "Paid in full" across her fine. It was he who set her free.

Her father was wounded for her transgression. Her father was bruised for her iniquities. Her father was grieved with her guilt. Her father bore the cost of her acquittal. By his substitutionary sacrifice on her behalf, she was set free, restored, made whole again as a member of his family and a member of society.

This little story is a true account of a single, sublime incident in the annals of a California courtroom. In the stirring saga of human history and God's sovereign dealing with the human race, we see the same precise principle at work.

The Lamb of God Gathers the Strays

The sixth verse of this regal chapter of Isaiah is without question one of the best known and most familiar in the whole of the New Testament. Millions have glibly quoted it across the centuries. Yet few pause long enough to seriously consider its enormous implications.

"All we like sheep have gone astray."

What does it mean to be like sheep?

What is it to go astray?

If the simile were truly understood, most men and women would be deeply offended. In our western culture, most people blithely assume that sheep are sweet, soft, white, innocent, harmless creatures dotting far-off hillsides, looking so inviting and cuddly in their woolly coats.

How far from reality! The harsh, unhappy truth is that sheep just aren't that beautiful—except at a distance and in the poetic imagery of the viewer's imagination.

Sheep are very, very stupid! They are incredibly stubborn! They have a very offensive odor. They are prone to sickness, susceptible to innumerable parasites and diseases. Timid, helpless, fearful creatures, they move under blind compulsion of the mob instinct. Under improper management when left to their own devices, they can be most destructive of the land and its resources. They are, when unattended, harsh and hardheaded with one another. They have a natural predilection to wander away, ending up in difficulties of a dozen kinds. They are easy prey for predators. They are a perpetual worry to their owners. No other class of livestock demands so much constant, meticulous care and attention.

No, sheep are not naturally attractive animals; and neither are we!

Man in his pride, arrogance and haughty intellectualism proclaims himself to be "homo sapiens"—the wise man. In the blindness and folly of his own supposed wisdom and philosophy, he insists that he is the ultimate product of the evolutionary process. This chance system, he argues, began purely by accident and proceeds by fits and starts with no specific design or direction. In ignorance, stupidity, and incredible perversion, man has gone on to proclaim that there is no God. He declares vehemently that because he is the product of pure happenstance, he need not answer to anyone for his conduct or behavior. Man, he insists, is but a molecular entity with chemical and physical responses to external stimuli. Ultimately, he states, each one is entitled to go where he may choose; to behave as he may wish; to do his own thing in his own way no matter what the consequences. "And every man did that which was right in his own eyes," could be our modern lament.

Are we surprised by the chaos and corruption of our society?

Are we surprised when Isaiah cried out in anguish, "We have *all* gone astray!"

In the realm of science and technology, men will respectfully submit to the disciplines of certain standards. An inch is an inch, whether it be in the Bureau of Standards in Washington, Tokyo or London. A pound is a pound, be it in Ottawa, Hong Kong or Canberra. Only as engineers, technicians, and tradesmen work and live by these basic standards can there be any sort of general cohesion of commerce and industry.

Yet in the realm of human conduct and personal behavior, men strongly resist any thought of a final absolute standard for their welfare and life. "Tolerance" is the watchword. It is believed that a person should be perfectly free to indulge any chosen life-style. The secularists claim that it is our inherent privilege to play life's little game by any set of rules we may devise or design.

Yes, Isaiah, we have gone astray!

We are astray not only collectively as a society, but we are astray as individuals within the family of man. To use the simple terminology of our Lord, the great Good Shepherd, we are "lost sheep."

Most of the men and women who turn their backs upon God, who ignore the call of Christ, who spurn the gentle overtures of His Spirit, do not realize the remorse and anguish they bring upon Him. In despising and rejecting Him, not only do they rupture their relationship with Him but also go on to ruin their own lives.

To turn to one's own way is really nothing less than to repudiate God.

Adding insult to injury, many behave as though God could be abandoned at will. We will just do our own thing and He will leave us alone.

Fortunately, is spite of the insistence of some that they have shaken Him off, it simply is not so. "Whither shall I go from thy Spirit?" asks the Psalmist. "Or whither shall I flee from thy Presence? If I ascend up into heaven, thou art there: if I make my bed in hell, behold thou art there. If I take the wings of the morning, and dwell in the uttermost parts of the sea; even there shall thy hand lead me, and thy right hand shall hold me. If I say, Surely the darkness shall cover me; even the night shall be light about me. Yea, the darkness hideth not from thee; but the night shineth as the day: the darkness and the light are both light to thee" (Psalm 139:7-12).

The whole question of being "near" or "far" from God, of being "lost" or "found," of being "astray" or "coming home," is not a matter of miles or distance in terms of spacial or physical measurement. Rather, it is a concept of closeness in which there is communion, agreement, harmony, mutual understanding and good-will between ourselves and God.

Two people may be sitting in the same room on the same couch together. If there is animosity, estrangement, ill will and misunderstanding between them, in truth they are "miles apart" even if they are within arm's reach of each other. So it is with us and Christ. The measure of our "closeness," our communion, our compatibility is not one of distance but of unity, agreement, love and mutual acceptance.

Incredible as it may sound, the responsibility for establishing this bond of affection and oneness between God and a sheep gone astray has been laid upon The Lamb of God. He it is who comes to seek and save the lost strays, to draw them back.

In the traditional life of the eastern shepherds, the stray sheep were always retrieved and gathered up by the shepherd's pet lamb. Every shepherd owned a special, hand-reared pet lamb who was considered almost as affectionately as his own children.

Like a veritable shadow, wherever the shepherd went, the pet lamb followed. Wherever he walked, the pet lamb walked. And whenever the shepherd set out into the wild pastures, the upland range or rough hill country to gather his stray stragglers, full responsibility for their safe return rested on the pet lamb.

It was the pet lamb who came alongside the lost ones, who fed side by side with them, who called to them, who influenced them to follow him gently back to the master's fold. It was the pet lamb, who, at the close of day as the sun set over the western hills, came home in the master's footprints, faithfully bringing the strays with him.

The term "bellwether" refers to this special lamb (who often wears a bell), bringing the stray sheep back to the fold, back to the shepherd. The divine Bellwether is The Lamb of God, Jesus Christ. Even out of the most difficult circumstances to which our own waywardness and selfishness have brought us, He gently but firmly nudges us in the right direction. In love and compassion and care, He comes to call us back to God our Father and home where we belong.

The Lamb of God in Silence

We westerners take great pride in our freedom to expound, propound, advocate, and articulate every thought, every cause which crosses our path. Thus the concept of a thorn-crowned Saviour standing silent before His accusers seems totally absurd to the modern mind.

This aspect is emphasized by the prophet as he likens The Lamb of God to a sheep struck dumb before its shearer.

Shearing sheep is not a sweet, romantic task. It is terribly hard work. It is done at the hottest time of the summer season. Then the wool "rises" from the sheep's skin, allowing the shears to move swiftly and deftly through the outstretched strands, separating the fleece from the pelt.

Sheep hate to be sheared. They are terror-stricken but silent in their fear and apprehension of the ordeal. When taken in hand they rigidly stiffen their bodies, arch their necks, then bury their heads in the midriff of the one who bends over to shear them.

In its natural state, raw wool is not the shining, snowy-white soft substance that most people imagine. Instead, it is usually very dark and dirty, stained with soil, mud and manure. In some cases it will be caked with several pounds of dung from the sheep itself. The fleece is full of sticks, bits of weeds, burrs and assorted grass seeds that cling to the fibers. Often it is infested with ticks, mites, and other parasites that prey on sheep. The fleece is greasy and oily with lanolin, which, when it is hot, emits a most disagreeable and repulsive odor.

Only after the wool has been removed from the sheep, then thoroughly washed and cleansed from foreign matter, does it have the attractive appearance commonly held in our mind's eye. Raw wool in Scripture represents the outward expression of the inner life. In its natural state it stands for *self*; and as such it was never allowed to be worn by any of the priests who entered the holy place or offered special sacrifices of sin offerings (see Ezek. 44:15-18).

When Isaiah in his first chapter compared sin to scarlet and crimson, contrasting them with snow and wool, he was referring to wool which had been washed, thoroughly cleansed and made ready for the spinning wheel. One of the great paradoxes of Scripture is the exhortation to bring our sins to the blood of Christ for washing white as newly cleansed wool.

The Lamb of God in Humiliation

After our Lord had celebrated the last Passover supper with His companions, and after He had shared with them the wonderful truths recorded in John chapters 13-17, He led them out to the garden of Gethesmane where His ultimate humiliation was to begin. Because all the dreadful details of that despicable ordeal have been recounted in my book RABBONI, they will not be elaborated on here. Sufficient to say that in His lynching, abuse, mock trial, torture, flogging, and in the desertion of those closest to Him, we see not only the bestiality of human behavior, but we see also the grandeur of God.

The reasons for saying this are twofold. The first is because Jesus' contemporaries, bent on His destruction, thought only that they were dealing with a man, some carpenter from Nazareth. They had set themselves to silence Him. They cared not about the methods they used to finally crucify Him. They resorted to all the intrigue, falsehoods, deception and evil of which human beings are capable.

What they did not know, and most men still do not know, was that "Jesus of Nazareth" was "God of Heaven." They did not recognize Him as The Messiah, The Anointed One, The Christ who had come to save them—God himself. They refuse to see His deity demonstrated in what He did and what He said.

Even to this day, some who consider themselves Christians draw back from the concept that Jesus Christ is none other than God. The world out-and-out denies His deity. Every attack made upon His person, every charge levied against His credentials by the false cults of the world, every falsehood perpetrated against Him by the opposing forces of darkness are ongoing evidences of His eternal verity, His timeless truth.

If Jesus were not the Christ of God, He would long ago have been lost in the hazy mists of man's memory. Like false pretenders and crafty imposters across the ages, His record would have blown away in the winds of time.

But that did not happen! Despite the most concerted attempts of human society, human philosophy, human governments and human ignorance to obliterate His presence and power, He has become the dearest person in all of life to a hundred million hearts from centuries past to the present. His deity goes unchallenged by those who know Him as Saviour and Redeemer.

Isaiah declared that He would be taken from prison and from judgment—that He would be cut off out of the land of the living, stricken for the transgression of His people. Here was His remarkable willingness—even beyond that, His *intention*—to be made captive in our human condition, to be humiliated and falsely accused, incarcerated in the narrow confines of our humanity. This He did, not by compulsion or constraint from without, but by His own choice: "It *pleased* the Lord to bruise him. . . ."

Jesus Christ was not a martyr. He who was subjected to such gross humiliation by His contemporaries was not merely caught in the toils and terror of fickle fate. He was, rather, God deliberately setting aside His honor, prestige, and splendor. The Eternal One quietly stripped himself of His own power to take upon himself the mantle of a man in human flesh and form. The everlasting *I Am* set aside His endless immortality to enter the captivity of an earthbound body subject to death. The Supreme Sovereign of the universe *made himself* of no reputation to become a suffering servant, The Lamb slain for our sins (Phil. 2:1-8).

> It was not men who bound Him against His will—it was He who chose to be made captive in our stead.
>
> It was not for His own wrongs that He suffered—it was for our sins that He was shackled.
>
> It was not His condemnation that took Him to the cross—it was our conviction that caused His death.

Even Pilate, looking at Jesus through the narrow, secularist view of a Roman official, could see this fact. He insisted, "I find no fault in Him." And the Roman governor's wife was fully aware that "this is an innocent man." The rough, tough, battle-hardened centurion who crucified Jesus exclaimed in awe, "Truly, this was the Son of God."

This willing Captive could proclaim liberty to the captives and the opening of the prison to them that are bound. He had been there!

He who made His grave with the wicked could forgive the wicked. The one whose body was bruised and beaten could bring healing to all mankind. In bearing the grief of His separation from God that day, He could bring comfort to those who sorrow. This One who carried the guilt of the whole world could bring forgiveness and reconciliation to all who would receive it. His captors shouted at him in derision, "He saved others, himself he cannot save!" Himself he *would not* save. If He had, all the rest of us would have perished. Yes, He was willing to be made captive, willing to be condemned, willing to be crucified in order that you and I could be set free, pardoned, and given eternal life.

Unshackled from bondage to Satan, sin, and selfishness, we are free to become His own humble "loveslaves," followers of The Lamb.

Part Two

The Lamb of God in Person

"When the fulness of the time was come, God sent forth his Son, made of a woman, made under the law, to redeem them that were under the law..." (Gal. 4:4,5).

Chapter Seven

The Lamb of God Incarnate

The Redeemer Comes

When Christ came, born of a virgin—the Eternal One, the Prince of Peace, the Mighty God, the Everlasting Father, the Wonderful Counselor—He set aside His supernatural splendor. In unutterable condescension He humbled himself, took upon His impeccable person the form of a man. God himself entered the human family as a babe born at Bethlehem (Isa. 9:6; Phil. 2:1-11).

Here was the supreme Seventh Act.

For some thirty-three years He would play His divine role upon the planet garbed in human guise. Most of His contemporaries were totally oblivious to His origin. They understood even less of His purposes in this performance.

Even His so-called earthly "parents," in reality but His boyhood guardians, scarcely seemed to grasp the fact it was not only the Son of Man who had come into their care but also the Son of God. His behavior as a boy baffled them. At the age of twelve, He stunned even the teachers and scholars steeped in the traditions and ancient truths of Israel.

This little lad who ran and played and laughed and cried and asked a score of searching, stabbing questions of His mentors was no ordinary child. He was *The Lamb of God* moving among ordinary men in mufti. He grew in grace with both God and man. But His family and friends really knew Him not. Though maturing in favor with His fellows, still He stood among them as a stranger from another sphere.

The days of His youth and early manhood were busy with boyhood exploits and the usual achievements of human adolescence. He was not a difficult teenager, given to tantrums and sullenness. Rather, He honored His lowly peasant parents, taking on the trade of a simple, small-town carpenter.

Working with wood; sawing planks; shaping slabs of timber; smoothing yokes; building boxes; making plows; hammering spikes and chopping chunks of tough olive wood or handling heavy acacia were part and parcel of His earthly drama and youthful days.

The pungent aroma of fresh cedar sawdust, the smooth feel of oak shavings curling over His big brown hands, the beautiful grain of freshly smoothed wood were the greater portion of His few short years, so simply spent in the carpenter shop.

Though He was The Lamb of God, the Everlasting One, His neighbors were the rough-and-tumble tradesmen of Nazareth, a tough trading town. It stood on the crossroads of commerce that criss-crossed the country. Here shepherds and farmers and camel drivers and common city people came to Christ, not to have their souls and spirits mended but broken beds and worn-out plows and cracked yokes.

He knew all about making candlesticks and ox stalls and shepherd crooks and farmer's forks. He was God, very God, in close touch with man, very man. Out of all these personal, private contacts came the great parables, the timeless truths, the pungent, powerful teaching of His later public ministry.

Then one day the whole scene changed. He set down His saw; hung up His hammer; put the plane on its shelf; dusted off the sawdust from His hands and headed for the distant Jordan River.

As He moved down the slope leading to the water's edge where John, the flaming desert fire-brand, stood shouting to the masses around him, Jesus was noticed. For the first time in almost thirty years of quiet obscurity, His true identity was recognized. John, the most powerful prophet ever to appear in Israel, shouted aloud for all to hear and see— "Behold, look, there is The Lamb of God!"

John's dramatic announcement seemed, for the most part, to be lost on the careless crowd. A tiny handful of his own disciples eventually felt drawn to follow Christ. But out of the multitudes of thousands whom John baptised, never more than about a hundred ever felt the personal compulsion of Jesus of Nazareth. Even at that, almost all of these eventually deserted Him. Ultimately, only a faithful band of a dozen tough, young teenagers were in His regular retinue. Of these the oldest was the blustery, big fisherman, Simon Peter, whose forceful personality eclipsed most of his mates.

For nearly three years the little band of thirteen men roamed and ranged like wandering sheep across the length and breadth of Palestine. Their Bellwether was Jesus of Nazareth. Though the rambunctious young roustabouts scarcely realized it, they were following God in human guise.

Awe-struck, sometimes startled, other times deeply dismayed, they imagined somehow their hero would usher in a powerful new empire of which they would be an important part. His constant reference to His new and unique "Kingdom of God" was a theme that fired their youthful zeal and charged their latent ambitions to break out from the bondage of Rome. They would be glad to get rid of the Caesar's legions. They would be happy to see Pilate sent packing.

Yet His way of going about such grand schemes puzzled and perplexed them. He never established a power base for himself. He never formed any political party. He never forged any links with the ecclesiastical heirarchy of the day. He never made any attempt to manipulate people. No committees were commissioned to make a study of the current economic climate. He never used any subtlety or diplomacy to try and ingratiate himself with those in positions of power or prestige.

On the contrary, this Christ was a loner. He was an enigma to His contemporaries. He was a scourge to the so-called spiritual leaders of His day. He was a menace to the status quo of His society.

Wherever He went, the impact of His person and the dynamic of His teaching attracted enormous public interest. Men and women by the multitudes came to Him for healing of body, for cleansing from disease, for delivery from demons, for restoration of sight, for uplift of spirit, for refreshment of soul, for forgiveness of sins.

The lives He touched were turned around. The eyes He looked into, with such enormous love, beheld the beauty of God in this One, yet most of them knew Him not. He was The Lamb of God moving amongst the lost sheep of the nation of Israel, bringing back a few strays from their self-willed wandering.

Repeatedly and emphatically He stated that He had come to seek and to search and to save the lost sheep that had strayed.

The way an eastern shepherd did this was always by using his own pet lamb to lead the wanderers home. Here was The Lamb of God playing this very role amid lost and weary men and women. He had come unto His own, but most of His own had not received Him, much less responded to His overtures of compassion.

Often He looked out on the careless, milling multitudes around Him. "Oh," He cried from the depths of His sorrowing spirit, "they are like sheep that have gone astray, lost and bewildered without a shepherd" (See Matt. 9:35-38).

Not only did He do His utmost to gather up a few, but He sent out His twelve young companions in pairs to do the same. "I am sending you out to the lost sheep of Israel," He told them. "You will be as sheep among wolves, terribly vulnerable, dreadfully endangered; but be of good courage, I shall be with you" (Matt. 10).

It was all very exciting, very blood-tingling, very daring and dramatic. They too, like their leader, healed the sick, restored sight to the blind, cast out demons, and even considered burning up whole communities with celestial fire if they failed to grant them a proper reception.

Sometimes their short-sighted and impetuous tactics did not mesh with The Master's way of doing things. They were looking for fireworks, action, and visible results. He seemed intent only on quiet service and utter self-sacrifice.

In fact, some of them became incensed with His attitude of love and concern in ministering to the endless needs of men and women. It mattered not what their demands might be, whether for food or forgiveness or teaching or healing. Jesus was always ready to give and give and *give* of himself. In contrast, His companions complained that the crowds should just simply be sent off home; there was a limit to how much a man could endure.

What they did not seem to know was that this "man" with whom they tramped over the dusty trails of their tough land was "The Man of Sorrows"—God himself touched with the feelings of human infirmity. He was moved by the sin and pain of struggling mankind.

And as He himself moved steadily, surely, with unshaken step toward an almost inevitable confrontation with His enemies, His disciples were utterly bewildered. Stormy, sullen, passionate Peter even tried to prevent it happening. In frustration he shouted at Jesus that this should never take place.

But it was for the cross that He had come! The horrible hounding of His footsteps; the cruel, relentless attacks on His person and teaching; the final explosive confrontations with the ecclesiastical hierarchy of the day; the stirring triumphal entry into Jerusalem; the moving last supper with His men; the agony of Gethsemane; the bestial betrayal; the mock trial by those in power—these were all but a dramatic prelude to the cataclysm at Golgotha.

In all of this anguish, Christ moved with quiet strength and calm serenity. Nothing, nothing, took Him by surprise. Though He was "the Man of Sorrows," acquainted with grief—both ours and His—He was also "The Lamb of God," moving in might and majesty.

It was for the cross that He had come. It was for the sins of the whole world that He was to suffer. He was The Passover Lamb, slain, suffering from before the foundation of the world, absorbing the penalty for us all. It was our perversity, our pride which would take Him to the tree. In this perfect Being there was no fault. He was The Lamb of God, blameless, harmless, impeccable in conversation and action. He, the faultless One, the sinless One, the innocent One, alone could stand and suffer and die in our stead, without a blemish.

Here was God in Christ, reconciling the whole world unto himself. Here was He who knew no stain or shame of sin, being made sin for us blighted mortals, that we might be made righteous with His very own righteousness (2 Cor. 5:18-21).

Yes, at this Passover feast, celebrated with such strong and emotional ardour by the unknowing multitudes, God acted to intervene on their behalf. He saved others; but in order to do so, himself he could not, dare not, save. The very essence of His character; the very make-up of His divine Person, demanded that He share His own life; lay down His own body; spill His own blood; give up His own Spirit in order to save us from our sins.

This was God's way. This was His Son's way. This was eternity's way. This was love's way. This is the way of the cross.

Those who stood and looked upon His dying could not understand. Nor do most of us!

In utter blindness, ignorance and folly the society of the day laid cruel hands upon The Lamb of God, offering Him as a substitute for subversive Barabbas, a man given to violence and intrigue. The mob thought it a joke of sorts. They screamed for the innocent blood of an innocent man, little knowing how desperately their depraved souls needed that blood to cleanse and purge them from their own poisonous iniquity.

In their shame and stupidity men have ever crucified God to assuage their own conscience. Always, ever, they insist it is God who is wrong, God is at fault, God is to blame for their own wicked behavior. It is God who is nailed to the cross of their sinful conduct while evil wears the crown in all of their affairs.

As Christ hung on the cross, the crowds clapped their hands in glee. They jeered at His plight and pain. They scoffed as though He were nothing more than a scarecrow suspended on a hill between heaven and earth. Little did they know that as His Spirit was given up, He entered the hell of separation from His own righteousness in order that they might be clothed in His own holiness.

It was a dramatic, earth-shaking transaction.

It was translated into terms of sorrow and suffering for all the world to see . . . but beyond human comprehension.

For sin and cynicism had blinded those who looked on with contempt.

Only the rough, battle-hardened Roman Centurion and his elite guard looked upon The Lamb of God in brokenness of heart and contrition of spirit. They cried out from the depths of their spirits:

"Surely this was the Son of God!"

Only God could lay down His life with such royal dignity for such contemptible humanity.

Such amazing condescension is almost beyond my puny ability to grasp. Such incredible humility is beyond my capacity to understand. Such awesome compassion for lost sheep like myself is beyond my hard heart to resist. From out of the depths of my innermost being there is wrung the cry, "You came, Christ, You came because You cared!"

It is this One who grew up in Galilee. It is this One who for so many years toiled in the relative obscurity of a dusty carpenter's shop in Nazareth. It is this one who as a tender lambkin ran errands for Mary and Joseph, leaving little footprints in the the dusty paths of His hillside town and in the hearts of His family and friends.

The Scriptures are very meager in their record of these early years of Our Lord's life. But in the brief and abrupt statements that are made there is a precise endorsement of the ancient prophet's pronouncement. He, The Lamb of God, would and did grow up in favor both with God and man. He matured in both wisdom and stature. His teenage years and adolescence were not marred, not marked by hostility, arrogance or tempestuous rebellion. He was a well-adjusted youth.

Yet, in spite of all this, His contemporaries saw nothing of unusual or special significance in Jesus the carpenter, son of Joseph. His fellow townsmen from Nazareth looked upon Him as one of their excellent craftsmen. He learned His trade well from Joseph. He did careful, meticulous work, with skill and expertise of the highest caliber. Any yoke He made or chest He built was bound to wear well and last for years.

In the process of time, He came to be well known

as the carpenter's son. He was commonly called Son of Joseph. He was considered, after His father's untimely death, as "The Carpenter." If one wanted first-class workmanship at fair prices, delivered on time, done with dignity, Jesus was the "man" to do it.

Before His Galilean neighbors and associates Jesus was a pleasant, quiet, unostentatious bachelor whom children loved and adults were content to regard as their friend. But beyond this He had no special or unusual magnetism that marked Him out as one of God's special appointment.

Before God, however, this One living out His early years in the degradation of Nazareth was His Son, His Lamb, garbed in the guise of a carpenter.

If ever there was a town in the hills of Galilee greedy for gain, it was Nazareth. It was to Galilee what Las Vegas is to the U.S.A. or Havana is to Cuba. Nazareth was where the fierce passions of foreign traders crossed with the deceitfulness of crafty merchants.

It was a town notorious for its pimps, prostitutes and evil of a hundred sorts. Here there were imported all the lewd practices of Phoenicia, Persia, Rome and the pagan tribes of Palestine.

Amid such sordid surroundings, this veritable wasteland of wickedness, the Lamb of God left His first footprints in the dust of time.

His contemporaries had no special respect for this "suffering Servant" who toiled at His common trade among them. But God did. He saw Him as His only begotten Son, the first among many brethren.

Few of us ever fully comprehend the soul anguish of the sinless Son of God during His dreadful years in Nazareth. What torment of spirit, what anguish of heart, what suffering of soul He endured as He grew up before God amid such evil! It is indeed astonishing that the divine record is so silent on this span of time in which He endured such contradictions of sinners.

The whole atmosphere of Nazareth, its environment, its life-style, must have been a horrible affront to His impeccable person. Perhaps it is well for us that the shades of silence have been drawn across these formative years of Christ's early manhood.

Certainly during His youth He was never singled out as someone very special by His fellow Galileans. In His early manhood He was never lionized as a potential leader. He was never elected to any position of prominence. He was simply regarded as "one of us"—"the carpenter of Nazareth."

Apparently only His mother, Mary, knew and hid away in the depths of her own spirit the special knowledge that this, her firstborn son, was also God's special Son. She sensed that her lamb was also God's Lamb.

And when, after thirty long years of waiting in the wings, the day finally came that He stepped for the first time into public view, John the Baptist shouted—"Behold, The Lamb of God!" When He rose from the Jordan waters a voice from Heaven declared—"Thou art my Beloved Son; in thee I am well pleased!"

This is the One of whom the prophet Isaiah 700 years earlier had declared:

> "For unto us a child is born,
> unto us a Son is given;
> And the government shall be upon His shoulder:
> And His name shall be called:
> Wonderful,
> Counselor,
> The Mighty God,
> The everlasting Father,
> The Prince of Peace" (Isa. 9:6).

Here was God himself, bearing all the splendor, all the attributes, all the titles of the Triune Godhead, stepping out in the public manifestation of His own Person, yet in the form of a perfect man. This is a concept which escapes most of us to this day, even with the full benefit of our historical hindsight and increased illumination.

This tender, unpretentious, unostentatious "Lamb of God," declared so fearlessly and forthrightly by John to have come taking away the sin of the world, was no less than God the Father, God the Son, God the Holy Spirit–in His completeness, in His might, in His majesty.

Yet to His contemporaries, Jesus the Christ remained but another mendicant without any special magnificence, without any unusual magnetism, without any unique material attributes that would attract others to Him.

It is true, as we shall see subsequently, that He often had crowds of people pressing in upon Him. Yet this was never because of His personal appeal or charming charisma. Children, it is said, were attracted to Him because of the integrity of His character and gentleness of spirit. But the massed multitudes came either to be fed, to be healed, to see the miracles or to have their hope of an earthly empire ignited by His teaching concerning the Kingdom of God, which few ever understood.

This was proven by the manner in which gradually His public life slowly sank into obscurity, until at the end He was forsaken by all.

All of this entailed enormous suffering for the Saviour. Anything worthwhile in the world always costs a great deal. Our deliverance, our redemption from our own despair, our liberation from our own dilemma have been paid for at the appalling price of God's own terrible reproach by men.

Let us never delude ourselves into thinking that The Man of Sorrows shared our sorrows lightly or bore our grief with gaiety. He was not just a jolly good fellow. He was not participating in a pantomime.

He was, instead, shot through with the pain and pathos or our human tragedy. He entered fully and completely into the trauma of His times. Not only did He bare the slings and stones of adversity hurled at Him by His antagonists, but in a second deep dimension He drank to the dregs the despair of our human condition.

Unlike the God of any other world religions concocted by the contrivance of man's imagination, this

One came among us in total identification. He walked where we walk. He stood where we stand. He lived at our level. He was tested at all points as we are tempted. He made himself one of us. He understood us completely. He who knew no sin was made sin with our pollution that we in turn might be made right with His righteousness (2 Cor. 5:19-21).

He had never known such ignominy in the realms of Glory whence He came. For there He had moved in an environment free from the stress, the sin, the darkness and despair of our human condition. Yet let it never be forgotten that there, too, He had been fully aware that He must share our sorrows and be fully cognizant of our grief.

Otherwise He could never be our God.

Otherwise He could never be our Strong Deliverer.

Otherwise He could never be The Lamb of God that takes away the sin of the world.

Yet, strange as it may seem, impossible as it may sound, despite all He has done on our behalf, we turn our faces from Him, not wishing to be identified with Him.

It is well nigh incredible.

It is so true it can hardly be taken in!

It is the most incongruous ingratitude known on earth.

The world as a whole does not honor or esteem Christ as someone special or worthy of acclaim. He is regarded with disdain as someone meek and weak. He is put down as someone pathetic. He is made of no account with ridicule, jests, and cruel jeers.

His name is bandied about by millions in profuse profanity and loathsome oaths. His dignity is dragged in the dust by thousands who think it great sport and very cunning to hold Him in contempt and scorn. Blatant books and scandalous films are produced to portray Him as a pervert or false pretender.

No other god in all the world is attacked with such vehemence or vituperation. He is the object of an on-going lampoon by those whose own lives are sordid and sunk in debauchery. The assaults of man against this One have never abated. And it will be seen that they will be accentuated. He is not esteemed except by those few who have learned to know Him and love Him.

Yet, let me remind the reader, that though men have done such dreadful despite to The Lamb of God, He in turn has never turned against us. He has never returned railing for railing. He has never reciprocated in anger against those who rejected Him.

Rather, His response has ever been, "Father, forgive them, for they know not what they do!" What an incredible attitude of generous grace! What a great God!

Dare we do less than quietly contemplate such compassion, such care, such concern; then, in turn, declare boldly, gladly: "I am one of His, I too shall share His suffering in this world."

The Lamb of God—Our Suffering Substitute

It is the man or woman who, through the illumination and conviction of God's own Gracious Spirit, sees themselves as a "sinner" who will seek His mercy. Because of the inherent pride of the human spirit, because of the innate perverseness of the soul, because of the incredible pollution of mankind most of us react violently against any mention that we may have wronged God.

The suggestion that we are surely sinners—that our selfish, self-centered behavior is diametrically opposite to the gracious, self-giving, self-less character of Christ—eludes most of us. Our excuse is, "That is how *everybody* thinks. This is how *everybody* behaves. That is how *everybody* lives."

It has not dawned on the consciences of most men and women that their whole life-style is an affront to God. It has not become apparent that both their inner attitudes as well as their outer actions have alienated them from the close companionship of a loving Father who longs to establish an open, intimate, joyous relationship with us as His children.

"Your iniquities have separated between you and your God, and your sins have hid his face far from you. . . ." (Isa. 59:3).

Perhaps if we put this problem into the perspective of an inter-personal human relationship, we can grasp what it is that we are doing to God.

Have you ever tried to live in the same home where one person was a proverbial liar? You discovered that this individual distorted the truth at every turn. You found nothing that was said could be relied upon with confidence. You learned that this one was usually deliberately misleading you.

Obviously an overwhelming alienation and separation would set in between the two of you. The other could not be trusted. His or her conduct and character would become a source of intense irritation. You would be injured, grieved and hurt by this behaviour. The other person would perpetrate lies about you; cast doubt upon your good character; circulate falsehood about your family; destroy your peace of mind; ruin your relationship with others; enmesh you in constant controversy.

All of this because this individual was given to lying and deception. This one defect alone would be enough to destroy any hope you might have of establishing a noble, wholesome relationship.

And yet there really is one hope for healing between you. There does remain one way of restoring harmony. A path of painful restoration is open to you.

It is the formidable force of forgiveness.

If you are the person great enough in spirit, generous enough in soul, good enough in heart to absorb these hurts; to take this abuse; to suffer these insults without rancor or recrimination, in time a bridge can be built between you and the offender.

The cost of such forgiveness is enormous. The suffering you must endure to extend forgiveness to your antagonist is heart-wrenching.

The hurts you personally must handle and the abuse you must absorb at the hands of your adversary are awful and awesome.

Yet this is the path of peace. This is the route to

total restoration. This is the highway to healing and wholeness—both for you and for the one who wrongs you.

Forgiveness, whether between man and man; man and woman; man and God, entails immeasurable cost. One must pay the price of personal humiliation.

This God has done, always does, ever will do in His loving, caring dealings with us.

May I remind you, dear friend, that our Father God does not reside "away out there" in the immensity of inter-stellar space. He is not some remote deity, isolated from our human condition, insulated from the sins and suffering which our human behavior imposes upon Him.

He is here.

He is present upon planet earth.

He is in immediate proximity to you as a Person at this point in time.

He is the One ever wounded with your terrible transgressions. He is the One bruised and broken by your wicked behavior, with your unbelievable craftiness. He is the One ever absorbing the blind and brutal outrages of your guilt.

This is The Suffering Lamb of God.

This is the One who instead of wreaking vengeance upon us for our vile behavior, absorbs the gross injustice of our conduct and extends to us the generosity of His own gracious forgiveness.

This is the One who, in the person of Christ, came among us, laying aside the power, splendor, and authority of His divine position, to make himself of no reputation; to stand all the abuse heaped upon Him; to absorb all the insults and degradation hurled at Him, in order to extend forgiveness to us fallen men.

Someone had to accept the death sentence for fallen man.

That One was God our Father himself, Judge of all the earth, Saviour of all lost men, who saw there was no other way to deliver us.

In the person of His Own Son, in the guise of human form, having set aside His glory in the eternal dimension of the heavenlies, the suffering Saviour stripped himself, stepped down to our place, and as The Suffering Substitute paid the price of the sin charged against us in order to deliver us.

No wonder total forgiveness has been granted to us.

No wonder complete reparation has been made for our wrongs.

No wonder utter reconciliation has been accomplished for us in the overwhelming, loving generosity of our Gracious God . . . Our Father in Heaven.

The Father and His Sons

During His short earthly sojourn among us in human form, Christ recounted the story of the father and his two sons. Though often titled "The Prodigal Son," its purpose was, and is, to portray the remarkable character of God. In ways more poignant and profound than any other parable it reveals what the forgiveness of God really is (Luke 15:11-32).

The young prodigal demanded his full share of his father's estate. This he promptly proceeded to waste and squander in total abandon. Flinging off all restraint, he "lived it up" without any sense of responsibility to his loving benefactor. That he debased himself in debauchery and drunkenness mattered not. His self-centered pre-occupation with sensual indulgence ultimately plunged him to the animal-like level of a boar in a pig pen.

In all of this it was his father who bore the burden of his behavior. His father knew full well what his son was doing. His father felt the anguish of his son's folly. He saw his own reputation dragged into the mud by his son's misdeeds. He suffered the excruciating pain of personal heartbreak over his boy's behavior. He endured the loss of much of his estate in his son's stupidity. He absorbed the personal humiliation of the prodigal's perversity. The dear man died a thousand deaths in suffering and sorrow for his willful, wayward son.

Yet never once did he turn away from him in disgust.

His tear-filled eyes searched that lonely, empty road leading home, waiting for his boy's return.

In his great, generous heart, forgiveness waited to be extended. It was always there. The price for this forgiveness had been paid. Its cost had been carried. All of its suffering had been endured long before ever the boy came back.

So, when at last, the crucial day came that the son

dragged his sin-stained, selfish soul back to his father's home, it was to be greeted not with reprimands and rebuke but with hugs, kisses, joy and delight.

This is forgiveness, the great forgiveness of God!

It was the father who had suffered and suffered and *suffered* in the place of the prodigal. It was he who had stood the shame. It was he who endured the loss. It was he who absorbed the humiliation.

But because of all this it was he and he alone who could extend healing to his boy. He alone could grant pardon. He alone could assure his boy of absolute acceptance again.

There was no re-hashing of the past. There was no going back into the mud and murk of his debauchery. There was no digging up of his degradation.

This is God's gracious, generous, great-hearted forgiveness.

Instead, the father flung a glistening white cloak around the shoulders of his son, completely covering the slime and shame of the pigpen. He thrust a new ring of gold on the hand that had squandered his estate. Here was total acceptance despite the worst his son had done to him. He placed new sandals on the mud-stained feet. From now on those feet would walk in new paths of peace and right conduct.

This is total forgiveness. This is total absolution. This is total acceptance. This is total healing between God and man, between heaven and hell, between Christ and me.

No wonder the fatted calf was butchered! No wonder a hilarious homecoming was celebrated with singing, dancing, and joyous music!

The one sad note in this startling story is that the elder, self-righteous, self-assured son never came in to join the festivities. His pride prevented this. He proved to be even more lost than his prodigal brother. He showed that his own selfish arrogance had alienated him from his father even more effectively than his brother's sinful behavior. Sin comes in many guises. Its most insidious form is selfish self-merit.

To both of his sons the father extended full forgiveness, full acceptance, full love. The prodigal son accepted this; but the elder brother would not.

When Christ told this story he was telling the story of His own love and forgiveness for us fallen men. Do you understand?

The Lamb of God in His Death

The death our Lord died was one of enormous depravity and indignity. It was part of the appalling humiliation to which He had subjected himself from the time of His entry into our human form.

From the crude, filthy manger to the cruel, ignominious cross, God in Christ had descended to the lowest depths to become identified with the lowest dregs of humanity. Many people are not prepared to face the appalling abuse heaped upon this One by the intransigence of His human contemporaries.

They try, instead, to draw a deceptive veil of respectability over the record of man's violent treatment of God.

In some cases cranks and cynics even portray Him as an imposter; a pretender; a charlatan who contrived His own crucifixion. All of which only proves the point even more dramatically of man's perversion and wickedness.

The truth—the terrible truth, the irrevocable truth—is that The Lamb of God, this One who suffered from before ever the earth was shaped and flung into space, was fulfilling in human flesh and form all that had been foretold for uncounted centuries. The dreadful, bestial abuse He underwent did not come as any surprise to Christ.

When He was betrayed by one of His closest friends and companions for thirty pieces of silver, He had been sold for the literal price of a slave; thirty shekels was the going price for a scrawny, black prisoner dragged to Jerusalam across the desert wastes from the Sudan, Ethiopia or East Africa. These wretched, weary, heart-broken fragments of the human family who had fallen into the terrible clutches of the slave traders were bartered away for thirty pieces of the bright metal. They were among the most forlorn of the earth's entire human community. Yet God in Christ reached down to their level.

His mutiliated form was manacled and beaten by His captors, and subjected to gruesome, ugly indecency. The ruffians off the streets of that fierce city of Jerusalem, the city that had always slain and tortured its prophets, pounced upon this One like hyenas and jackals dismembering a hapless victim.

He was stripped; He was spat upon; He was beaten; He was flogged with cruel whips bearing slugs of iron that gouged and tore His flesh; He was punctured with cruel thorns plucked from the desert and rammed down hard upon His head—all this evil was man's violent reaction against God's own unsullied righteousness.

It was the hatred of evil toward good.

It was the attack of depravity on truth.

It was the response of vileness to purity.

It was the reaction of sinful man against a righteous God.

His butchers came dressed in many guises. Some were the sophisticated scribes and scholars of the Sanhedrin. Others were the Pharisees, the High Priests and powerful ecclesiastical elite. Some who took part in slaying the spotless Lamb of God were ruffians off the dusty streets and side roads of this dreadful city. Some were royalty, garbed in robes of high office and supposed nobility. Still others were rough Roman soldiers, hardened in battle, tough in their games of human suffering. The conspirators came from every strata of society; they represented every segment of the world, the wretched, wicked world He had come to save.

Supposedly they had had their last laugh; when at last they were done with jeering and leering at Him; when finally they had wearied of their own terrible atrocities, they sat down to watch Him die.

This forlorn, forsaken Being hanging in appalling agony upon the tree was bearing not the burden of His own misdeeds but the incredible calumny of their own despicable misconduct.

It was not just the flaming, burning pain of spikes through His hands and feet; it was not just the loss of blood from gaping wounds in His brow, His back, His abused body; it was not just the tormenting thirst of dying by slow degrees beneath the burning sun that brought death.

It was the terrible, terrible load of sin that stained His sinless Person. This pure One, this sacred Lamb, suspended betwixt heaven and earth as the supreme sacrifice for all men of all time, was subjected to the shame of being made utter sin in our place.

From ancient times such an one was accursed of God. From the days of Moses, no greater indignity could be levied against any living soul than to be hung upon a tree. To be so degraded was to be despised and abhorred by both God and man. Such a death was considered to be so awful it even contaminated the countryside and defiled the very ground upon which the atrocity took place (see Deut. 21:22-23).

Under Roman rule, such spiritual observances were often set aside. Instead, the crows and ravens, vultures and carrion-eaters were allowed to consume the carcasses which hung on crosses. If any fragments fell to the ground, hyenas, dogs and jackals would scavenge them.

When soldiers came to check and see if the three

victims were dead, it surprised them to find that The Lamb of God had already expired; His Spirit had departed. So there was no need to shatter His shin bones as was the normal custom, that final awful shock used to terminate what little life might still flicker.

No, no bones were broken in the body of God's own Passover Lamb. And this too was precisely in accord with the divine edict of old. For in the institution of the Passover sacrifice, it was declared categorically that not a single bone should be broken. (Read Ex. 12:43-47; Num. 9:12).

In the gathering gloom of this horrendous day, two of Jesus' friends requested permission from Pilate, the Roman Governor, to take down the body. Their request was immediately granted—both because Hebrew custom demanded it, and also because it was Pilate's political stance to try to placate the religious leaders.

Previously that day he had made the ignominious exchange with them of Barabas for the brave "King of the Jews." But such grim exchanges are not uncommon among the children of men. People still play their ghastly little games with God. They still exchange life for death; light for darkness; love for despair—simply because their penchant for the evil things in life overrides any desire for decency... much less divinity.

To this very hour in human history men still shout, "Give us Barabas, give us knavery, give us violence, give us lawlessness! Away with Christ, away with honesty, away with righteousness, away with purity!"

Joseph and Nicodemus both were sure, as were His other disciples and the humble, heartbroken women who watched Him die, that this was the end of their friend and Master. The cross, they were sure, was the end of His career. His death meant the demise of their hopes and plans for the Kingdom of God.

How little any of them understood the events of the hour.

How few of us comprehend the triumph of Golgotha.

How few ever grasp the victory of God in His death!

It was not a man who gave his life on that cross. It was God, the Eternal One—*Love* himself.

That He tasted death there for every man is true.

But that death and decay could not constrain Him is seldom understood.

From the instant He declared triumphantly, "It is finished!" and volitionally freed His own Spirit from its imprisonment in human flesh and form, a path of utter freedom was fashioned for all men to follow.

For death could not hold Him!

For decay could not touch Him!

From birth up to His death He had been subject to the terrible degradation of our human condition. But at the moment of His resurrection He took to himself again all the splendor, power, majesty, dominion, glory and dignity of the Godhead.

When His friends wrapped His body in fine linen and special spices, these gestures were but human screen for the majestic movements of God in the unseen world.

He was alive! He was active. He was ministering to the multitudes of human spirits imprisoned prior to this hour. He was setting them free to follow Him, just as in subsequent centuries other imprisoned spirits, including yours and mine, could be freed to follow The Lamb of God, no longer bound by the shackles of death which He shattered for all time. (See 1 Pet. 3:18-20).

This One whom His friends thought they had interred in such a beautiful tomb was not wrapped in death. "He is not here!" the angel declared. "He is risen!" He whom men had treated with such violence and deceit had broken the bands of death. He had destroyed the fear of death. And now all men could pass through it . . . and beyond it, into the glorious realm of our God.

Surely, death was now but the doorway through which men could step into that new dimension of life with Christ.

He, The Lamb of God, had come; He had tasted death for every man; He had conquered; He had finished His earth work.

The resurrection of Christ has been an oft-neglected theme in the church. Yet at the time it happened, it transformed and galvanized a cringing, fearful little band as no other event could. The sudden, unmistakable, undeniable presence of the Risen

Lord was the tremendous thrust and divine dynamic of the early church.

No other human being in all of history has ever experienced a resurrection like this. It is true, men and women have been raised from death and returned to their previous pattern of mortal life. Jesus himself raised Jairus' daughter from death; He restored the son of the widow of Nain to his mother; He brought back Lazarus, His special friend, from the grave. And earlier in history, Elijah had restored the son of the widow of Zarephath to life.

Each of these and others like them have been resurrected from death. But here is the difference: each was still subject to death, still limited by time/space, still bearing a mortal body which would eventually fall under the power of death.

At Christ's resurrection, no man unwrapped His linen winding; no man commanded Him to rise again; no man removed the stone at His grave door; no man led Him forth from the grave.

When in majesty, might and splendor He stepped out of the human limitations of the form in which He had deliberately imprisoned himself for thirty-three years, it was to take on the resurrection form of *The Victorious Lamb of God.* No longer limited by time, space, matter, or human body, He could appear and disappear at will, moving with the unbelievable speed of light.

He could appear to the veiled eyes of His friends as a total stranger, a gardener, a companion on the road, a fellow fisherman on the beach. He could likewise be seen as their dearly beloved Master, Rabboni, their dearest Friend, the living embodiment of the One wounded with nails, punctured with thorns, pierced with a Roman spear—eating bread, tasting honey, relishing fish.

For forty days and nights He moved among His friends and followers in His wonderful glorified body. Eventually more than five hundred people saw Him. Here was The Lamb of God slain from before the foundation of the earth now appearing in resplendent resurrection form, understandable to human senses yet not restrained by the human condition.

"I am the resurrection and the life," He told Martha. The resurrection life which transformed His own body was the final stamp which validated and vindicated His life and death. This transformation more than any other single event brought His followers to a belief in Him that they had never had before.

One look into the empty grave, one moment's recognition of Rabboni's voice, one touch of His nail-pierced hands, one instant's breaking of bread, one breakfast by the beloved Galilee, and they all knew "it is The Master."

Everything now had fallen into place for them. All that He had said had been so; everything He told them had come true; The Lamb of God had indeed proven himself to be totally trustworthy, absolutely believable, utterly reliable.

Now all the spendid pageantry of His earthly sojourn was complete—every detail of its perfect execution carried out in accord with the sublime will and generous wish of God.

He had not resorted to violence to vindicate himself. He had not returned railing for railing to justify His own innocence. He had not tried to use His powers as the Potentate of heaven to manipulate men on earth. Not once had He deviated from the grand design to deliver us from our awful dilemma.

The Lamb of God had fulfilled and fully accomplished every prediction made about Him. All the ancient prophesies spoken of old by men, seers, priests and prophets under the unction of God's Spirit had been carried out to the most minute detail. He had totally verified all of the forecasts about His birth, life, death and resurrection amid the human race.

Now all of that was over. Now the splendid pageantry of His earthly sojourn was completed. Now the drama of His humanity was done. Every detail of its perfect execution had been carried out in accord with the sublime will and generous wish of God.

All of it was for our redemption, for our forgiveness, for our reconciliation to himself. All of this was stamped, sealed, and finalized by His remarkable resurrection.

By His perfect doing and by His perfect dying all the demands of the ancient, irrevocable, inviolate law of God were fully met. By His total, gracious, generous self-giving all the demands of a great, loving God were totally satisfied. By His magnificent substitution of himself in our stead, standing and suffering in our place, absorbing the penalty for our pride and rebellion He so brought us peace; and so our searching spirits and souls, too, are satisfied.

All He accomplished was achieved in utter perfection. All He did was in accord with the gracious, good, and generous will of God. He came. He conquered. He looked upon the terrible travail of His own soul, and He, too, was satisfied.

In all of this there was enormous glory, honor, and splendor surpassing what His friends could fully comprehend in those cataclysmic days. The rapidity of the events and the magnitude of the divine momentum left them almost aghast.

The giant, immaculate, shining linen curtain that had protected the privacy of the holy place in the Temple had been torn from top to bottom. No longer was the mercy seat of God an inviolate inner sanctum accessible only to the high priest once a year, even then only under the protection of the lamb's blood he bore in his hands. Now The Lamb of God himself had entered once for all into the most holy place. He had met man at the divine mercy seat. Now an open entrance for all men to come before the very throne of God without fear or apprehension had been made. The One who had been tempted in all points as we are, yet without sin, who had been touched with the feelings of our infirmities, now stood in power, majesty and splendor as our supreme Intercessor, our great High Priest. Even more wondrous, more startling, was the fact that The Lamb of God in resurrection assured a new relationship with himself. He called His followers His brothers. He told Mary to "go to my brethren, and say unto them, I ascend to my Father and your Father; and to my God, and your God."

The Lamb of God saw His humble, stumbling, unbelieving earth friends as "brothers." They had been brought into the family of God. They had been "adopted into the beloved." They had become heirs and joint heirs with Him. They were sons and daughters who had been lost and astray but now were in the fold. The Lamb of God had brought the wanderer's home. Some of the lost sheep were safe. He had brought sons to glory.

That Christ saw himself still active in this role is borne out by the last breakfast He shared with His brothers beside the lake. Though He helped them take in the largest catch of fish the young fellows had ever netted, their conversation did not center on fishing. Instead Jesus quickly turned to the topic of sheep.

Three times He questioned Peter closely whether or not he really did love Him. And three times the Lord instructed Peter carefully to care for His sheep and lambs. The joyous, hearty, happy days on the dear, old Lake of Galilee were over for all of them.

This was the beginning of a new era, a new age, a new dimension of responsibility. From now on The Lamb of God in glory would intrust to His brethren on earth the care and concern for other lost sheep. "As the Father sent me into the world, so send I you!"

The Lamb of God in His Ascended Majesty

An intense awe, a grand sense of wonder, a still,

profound touch of majesty attends our Lord's ascension. His return to the splendor and magnificence of the unseen realm was, on earth, but a momentary parting with His faithful followers.

One instant He was here: the next He was gone. There was no fanfare of trumpets to herald His departure. There was but the cloud overhead into which He was caught up to the heavens. Then came the simple, straightforward angelic announcement that one day He would return just as He had gone.

But what of the interim?

What transpired beyond the screen that separates the natural from the supernatural world?

We are told explicitly that He was crowned with glory and great honor. There was celebrated in the expanses of eternity a coronation that transcends anything man can imagine.

The Conqueror had come home!

The crown of command now rested on His thorn-pierced brow. The scepter of divine power was placed in His nail-pierced hands. His bruised body now reposed upon the throne of majesty on High. His pierced feet were placed on the footstool of His fame.

He who justified many and bore the guilt of multitudes now sits supreme in the realm of our God. As Paul put it so eloquently in his powerful epistle to the Philippian Church,

> "Wherefore God also hath highly exalted Him, and given Him a name which is above every name: That at the name of Jesus every knee should bow, of things, in heaven, and things in earth, and things under the earth; And that every tongue should confess that Jesus

Christ is Lord, to the glory of God the Father" (Phil. 2:9-11).

Well may we ask ourselves why we are not given greater details, further information? Simply because we could not possibly comprehend the magnificence of His might and majesty with our finite minds.

Sufficient for us to know that the glory and honor He set aside in order to take on himself our humanity, He now fully reclaimed and repossessed. The power and prestige which were previously His, He now re-assumed. He became again in very truth *King of Kings and Lord of Lords.*

Proof that this had taken place was the gift of His own power to His Church at the day of Pentecost. There came upon them the Mantle of His own gracious Spirit. Directly from Him by His own royal decree, they received the Paraclete who would empower the occupants of the Upper Room to go out and turn the world upside down.

The Lamb of God now reinstated in the heavenly places in great glory was the One worthy of all acclaim. It was because of Him and through Him and in Him that men and women drawn from every nation, tribe and tongue upon the earth would be formed into one family.

And their endless chant of praise throughout all of eternity would be, "Worthy is The Lamb that was slain to receive power, and riches, and wisdom, and strength, and honor, and glory, and blessing" (Rev. 5:12).

He it is who now holds in His hand the lives of

His own saints. He it is who keeps them from the evil one. He it is who grants to them the strength to overcome evil. He it is who empowers them to prevail against their own destructive self-nature.

To such His special sublime assurance ever remains:

> "To him that overcometh will I grant to sit with me in my throne, Even as I also overcame, and am set down with my Father in his throne" (Rev. 3:21).

It is the *person* of The Lamb of God in heaven which guarantees that there shall never again be any night there. Gone forever are the sorrows which comprise so great a part of our earth days. He, The Man of Sorrows, has long since borne them all away. Instead He now wipes away every tear, dries every eye, gives to His own the oil of gladness in the place of mourning.

It is in the *presence* of The Lamb of God in glory that all separation ceases. Never again will we be torn by the painful tugs of parting or the deep wounds of distance that so often distress us here.

The *power* of The Lamb of God guarantees the total extinction of all evil in His domain. Never, ever again shall sin or selfishness or evil hold sway. He has conquered all of these. He has subdued them to His sovereign purposes. His followers are set free in a new dimension of divine delight.

The *purity* of The Lamb of God assures us for all time that there can be no curse there. Nothing that defiles, deceives or diverts us from himself can enter there. Never again will His people have to contend with the wiles of the wicked one. The enemy of our souls will be banished forever, while the blood-bought children of The Lamb clap their hands with joy, giving glory, honor and adoration to Him who lives forever and forever.

He who is Potentate of the eternal ages will be seen at last as *The Lamb of God, The Alpha and the Omega, the one from everlasting to everlasting, who ever lives to make sublime intercession for us.*

In gratitude, awe and wonder His redeemed shall praise Him forever and serve Him with loyal devotion. *He is Lord of Lords, King of Kings, God very God!*

Amen and Amen!

Reflections . . .

It is with awe and wonder that we reflect quietly again upon the divine drama unfolded by The Lamb of God—Our Suffering Saviour.

Act 1—The personal intervention of Our Loving God to provide a proper covering for the wilful wrongdoing of the first man and woman, our federal forebears, Adam and Eve.—Genesis 3

Act 2—The substitute sacrifice of a lamb slain for the life of a single soul, Abel.—Genesis 4

Act 3—The divine provision of a suitable ram as a satisfactory sin offering for both father and son, Abraham and Isaac.—Genesis 22

Act 4—The arrangement by God for a pass-over lamb to provide protection for a whole household, a family and first-born son.
—Exodus12

Act 5—The sacrifice of a wilderness lamb, the scapegoat sin-bearer, to atone for the sins of an entire nation, Israel.—Leviticus 16

Act 6—The moving revelation to Isaiah of The Lamb of God suffering in the stead of all of us who have gone astray, each turning to his own way.—Isaiah 53

Act 7—The actual arrival, in human form, of The Lamb of God, God in Christ, to take away the sin of the whole world—Jew and Gentile—all men of all time.—Luke 2, John 1-3

GLORY BE TO THE LAMB!
—Revelation 5